ADVENTURES IN FLIGHT

THE EARLY
BIRDS OF WAR

THE EARLY BIRDS OF WAR

THE DARING PILOTS AND FIGHTER AIRPLANES OF WORLD WAR I

by

THOMAS R. FUNDERBURK

GROSSET & DUNLAP
PUBLISHERS NEW YORK

COPYRIGHT © 1968 BY THOMAS R. FUNDERBURK
ALL RIGHTS RESERVED
PUBLISHED SIMULTANEOUSLY IN CANADA
LIBRARY OF CONGRESS CATALOG CARD NUMBER: 68-12763
PRINTED IN THE UNITED STATES OF AMERICA

CONTENTS

1 EARLY BIRDS AND PENGUINS 13
2 "IT WAS TRAGIC..." 31
3 BLUE MAX 51
4 STORKS 67
5 RED BARON 87
6 "TARGET SURE" 103
7 VICTIMS AND VOLUNTEERS 117
8 COMPLETING THE CIRCLE 127
  Recommended Reading 151
  Index 153

THE EARLY BIRDS OF WAR

"There were men at Blenheim as good as the leader, whom neither knights nor senators applauded, nor voices plebian or patrician favoured, and who lie there forgotten, under the clods. What poet is there to sing them?"

WILLIAM MAKEPEACE THACKERAY
Henry Esmond, Book II, Chapter 25

1 / EARLY BIRDS AND PENGUINS

1

THE FIRST WORLD WAR, which was fought between the end of July 1914 and 11 November 1918, which cost eleven million lives and accomplished nothing, came about as the result of years of diplomatic distrust and frantic arms races between the major powers of Europe. The first overt acts of war occurred when the armies of Austria-Hungary invaded the Slav state of Serbia with the aim of redressing a long series of "indignities" by a crushing humiliation. Russia, as self-appointed protector of Slavic interests in Europe, immediately declared war on Austria. Germany, as ally of Austria, declared war on Russia. France, as ally of Russia, declared war on Germany. Faced with the prospect of war on two fronts, in France and Russia, Germany planned to deliver her blows first to knock one or the other of her adversaries out of the war before it could fairly begin. She planned to outflank the French armies and capture Paris within thirty-nine days, launching her invasion in the west with a wide-wheeling movement through the low fields of Flanders. She invaded Belgium in the process and brought Great Britain into the war against her, for Britain was pledged to fight to protect Belgium's neutrality.

It had all started because of fanatical nationalism and the resentment of "indignities."

The fuse was lit and the ensuing explosion ended the century of relative peace that began with the Treaty of Vienna in 1815, when the dismembering of Napoleon's empire had concluded the last continental war. It did more than that. The Great War of 1914–1918 completed the trap in which the world was caught again in 1939, and from which it has not yet escaped, the trap of blind nationalism and unreasoning political competition.

THE GREAT ARMIES that took the field in August 1914 numbered about six million men. France mustered sixty-two divisions, for example; Germany, eighty-seven. In the same month, France had one hundred twenty aeroplanes, not all of which were owned by the military and none of which were even military types. Britain had one hundred thirteen, and Germany had as many, precisely, as the two put together. This was decidedly a small beginning for military aviation.

The armies were not prepared for a war in the air because many of the military commanders believed that an inexpensive and limited war could be fought and won before Christmas. Many of them, when the shooting started in earnest in August, even believed that everybody would be home before the leaves turned. The old way, with elaborate general plans based on convenient assumptions and ignoring unpleasant realities, was the way the new war was to be conducted. And the old way, with sweeping corps movements and dashing cavalry charges, had no place for noisy, fussy, rickety, gimcrack aeroplanes.

What good were they, these contraptions, these flying machines? To tell the truth, they weren't much good. Not when we consider the endless and amazing variety of jobs today's aircraft can perform. The only thing they could do was carry a passenger—but that's all they had to do. If the passenger were a Regular Army man able accurately to interpret and report what he saw from the air, one aeroplane and its crew could do the work of a regiment of cavalry.

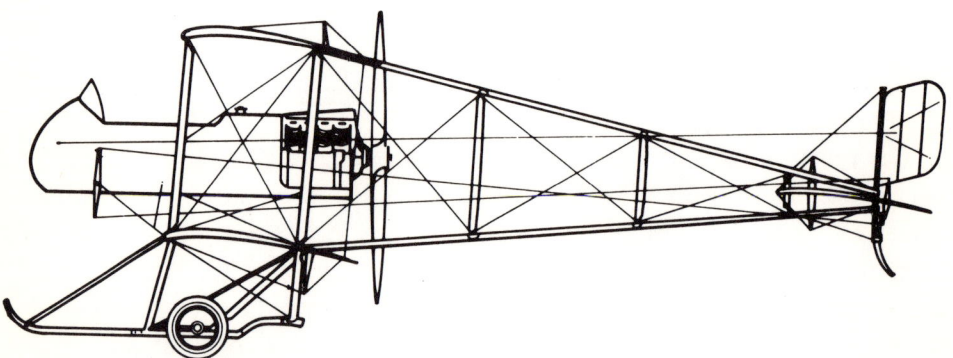

Maurice Farman "Shorthorn"

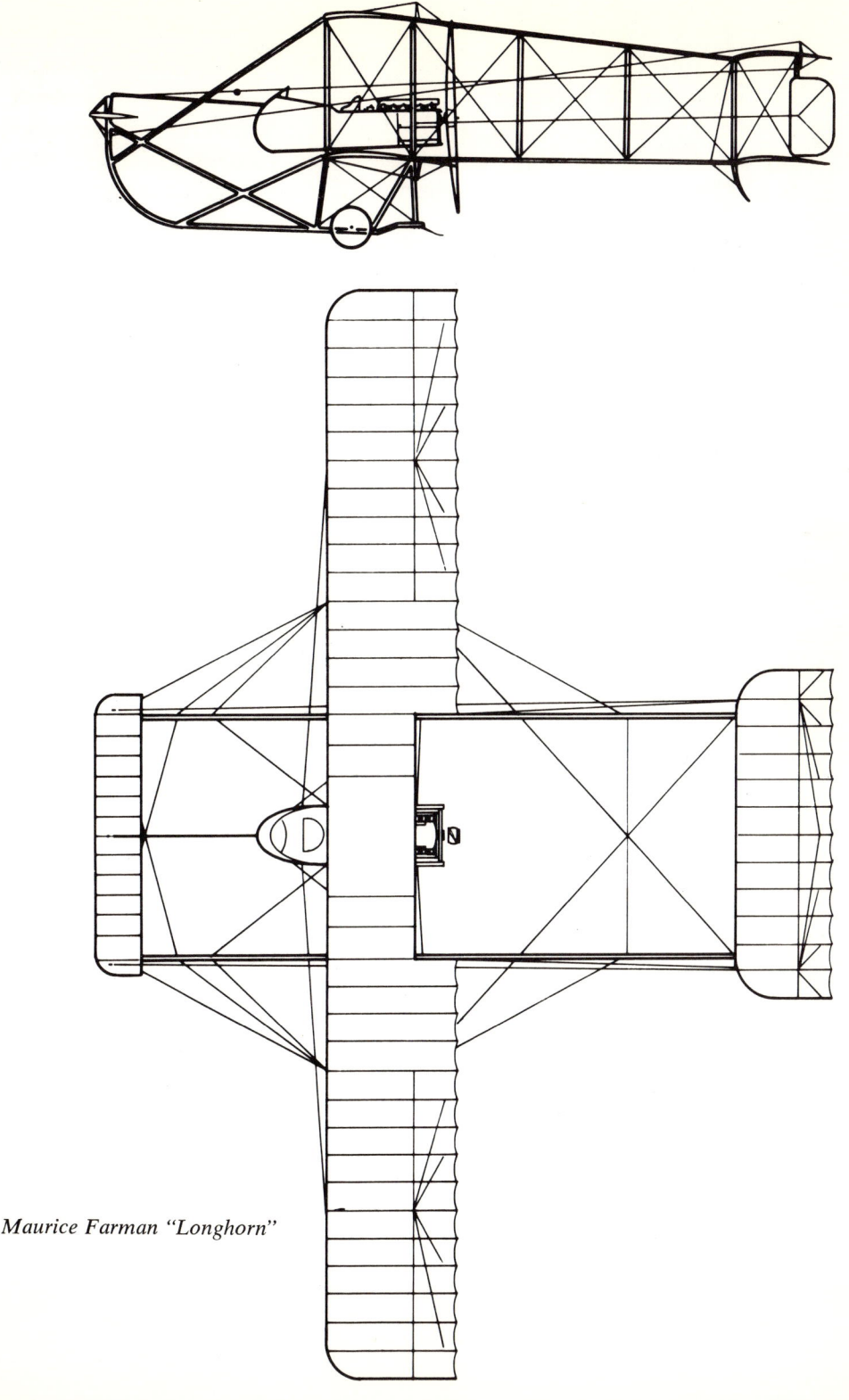

Maurice Farman "Longhorn"

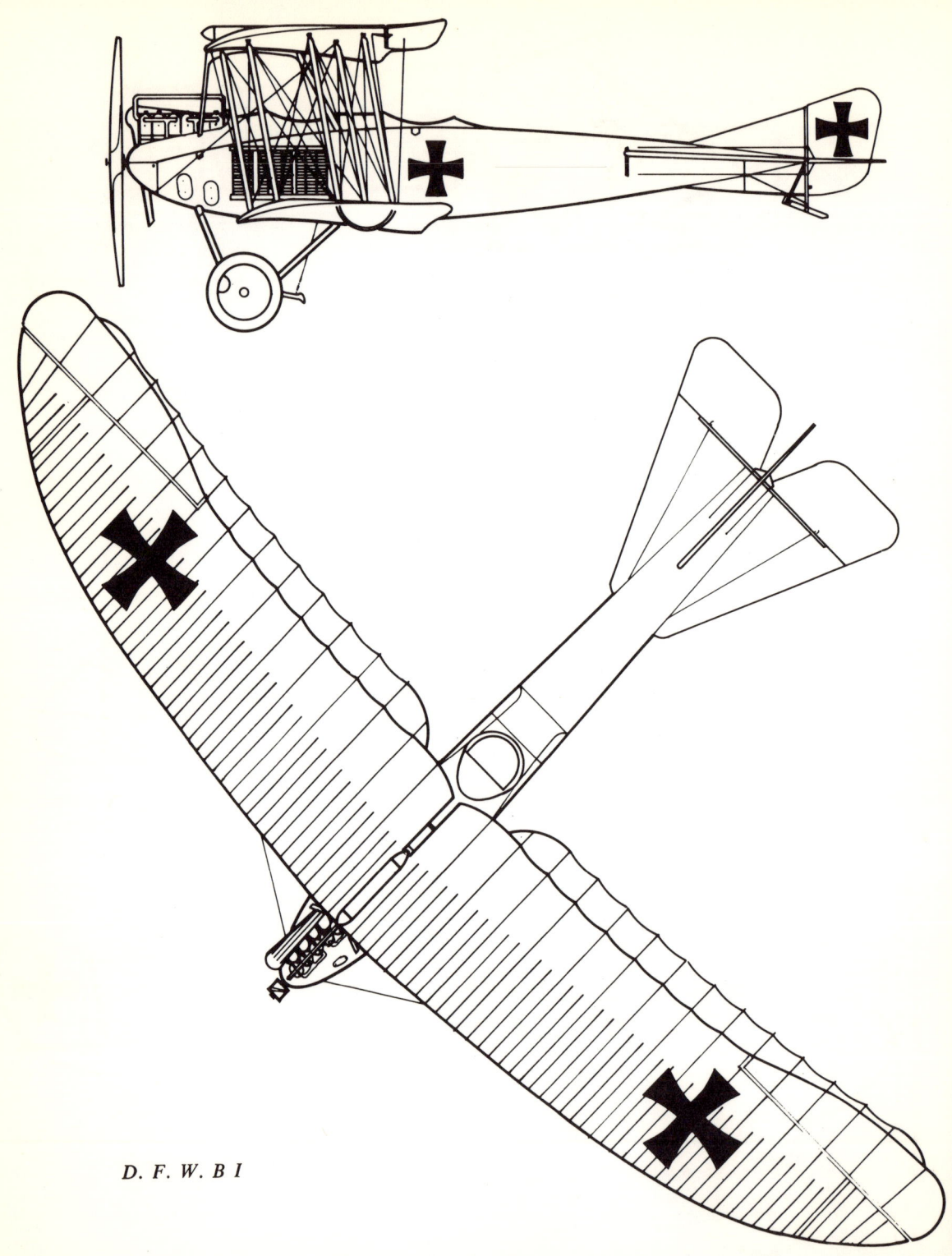

D. F. W. B I

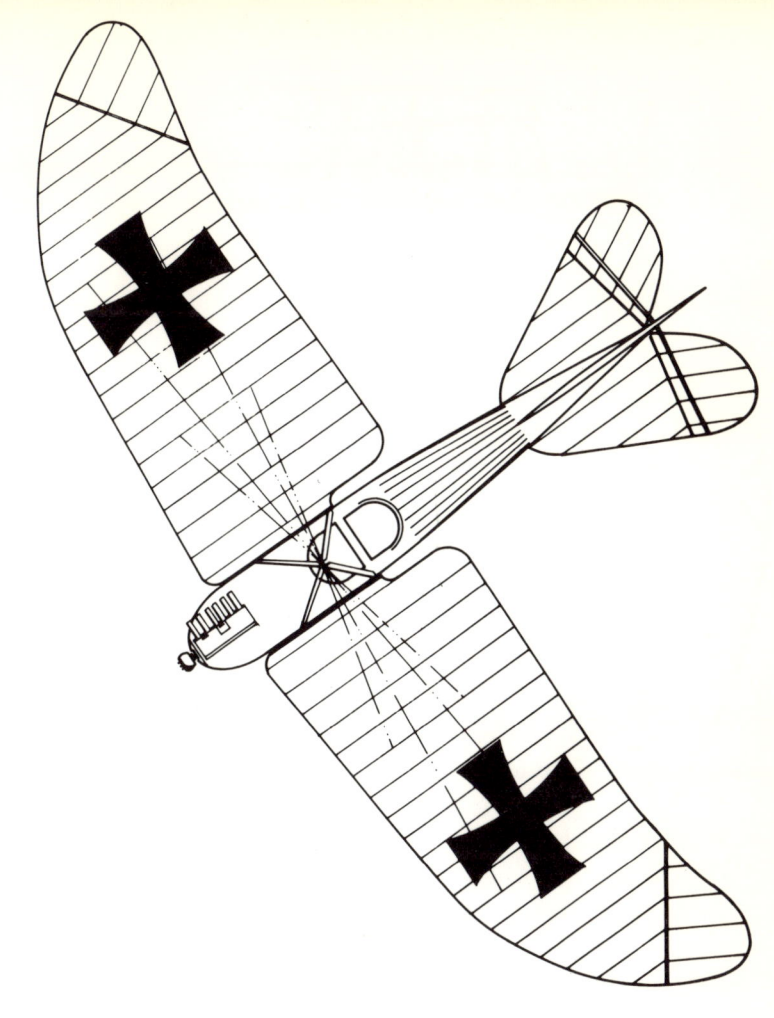
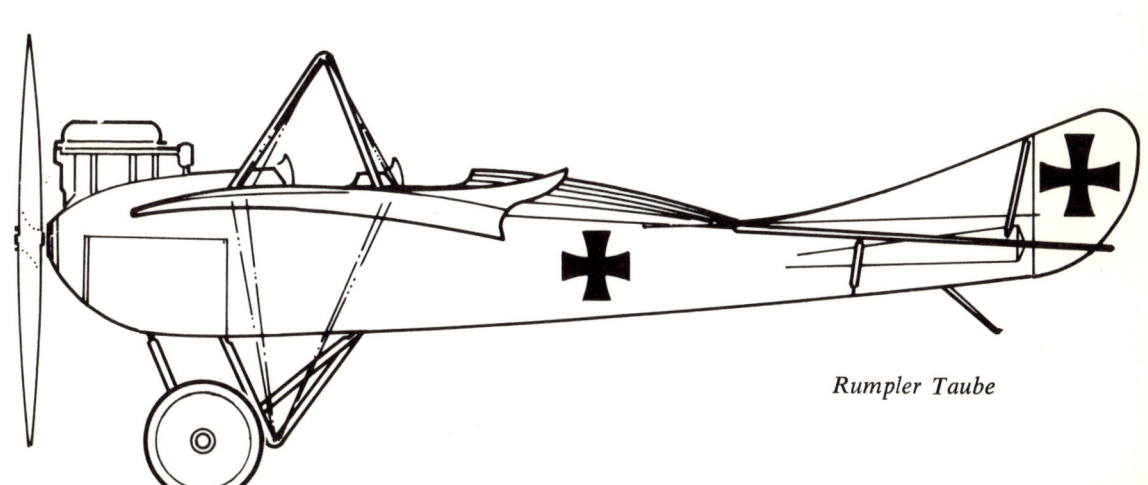

Rumpler Taube

Yet the areoplane had won only a limited acceptance when the armies had experimented with aerial reconnaissance before the war. For the commanders, the vision of wars being won in the grand old way was not to be forsaken lightly in the interest of a handful of greasy mechanics. When the nations went to war, the air services went along almost as an afterthought.

*   *   *

THE PIONEER AVIATOR, Louis Blériot, had flown across the English Channel in 1909 in a monoplane of his own design powered by a 35-horsepower Anzani engine. The aeroplane was the eleventh in a series of experimental designs and was accordingly named the Blériot XI. In the years after 1909, more powerful engines were devised and Blériot monoplanes with up to 80 horsepower were produced and sold to the military and to sportsmen flyers. One version of the original 35-horsepower machine was used by the French aviation service, the *Service d'Aéronautique,* as a primary trainer. This was called a Penguin, because it was a non-flying bird. Except for its clipped wings, however, it was the same as the machine in which Blériot had crossed the Channel.

An American who went through one of the Blériot schools was Charles J. Biddle, a Foreign Legion volunteer who could not wait for America to join the Allies. The French Foreign Legion was the usual way for men who were not French nationals to fight for France without relinquishing home country citizenship. Born 13 March 1890, Biddle was graduated from Princeton in 1911 and received a law degree from Harvard in 1914. Having been accepted for the *Service d'Aéronautique,* he was sent to the Blériot school at Avord, where he was enrolled in a class of *débutants,* or beginners, and started right out in a Penguin. Sitting in the cockpit he had a good idea of what it was like to sit in a real aeroplane. After a brief instruction on the motor and a few rudiments of flight, he fastened the safety belt across his lap and the motor was started up. When the chocks were removed from the wheels the machine rolled forward. All he had to do was ease the stick forward to lift the tail off the ground and work the rudder bar with his feet to keep the machine going in a straight line. When he had the "feel" of the controls and could stay on course, he was allowed to move on to the next

Louis Blériot (right) and an early pupil.

U. S. Air Force

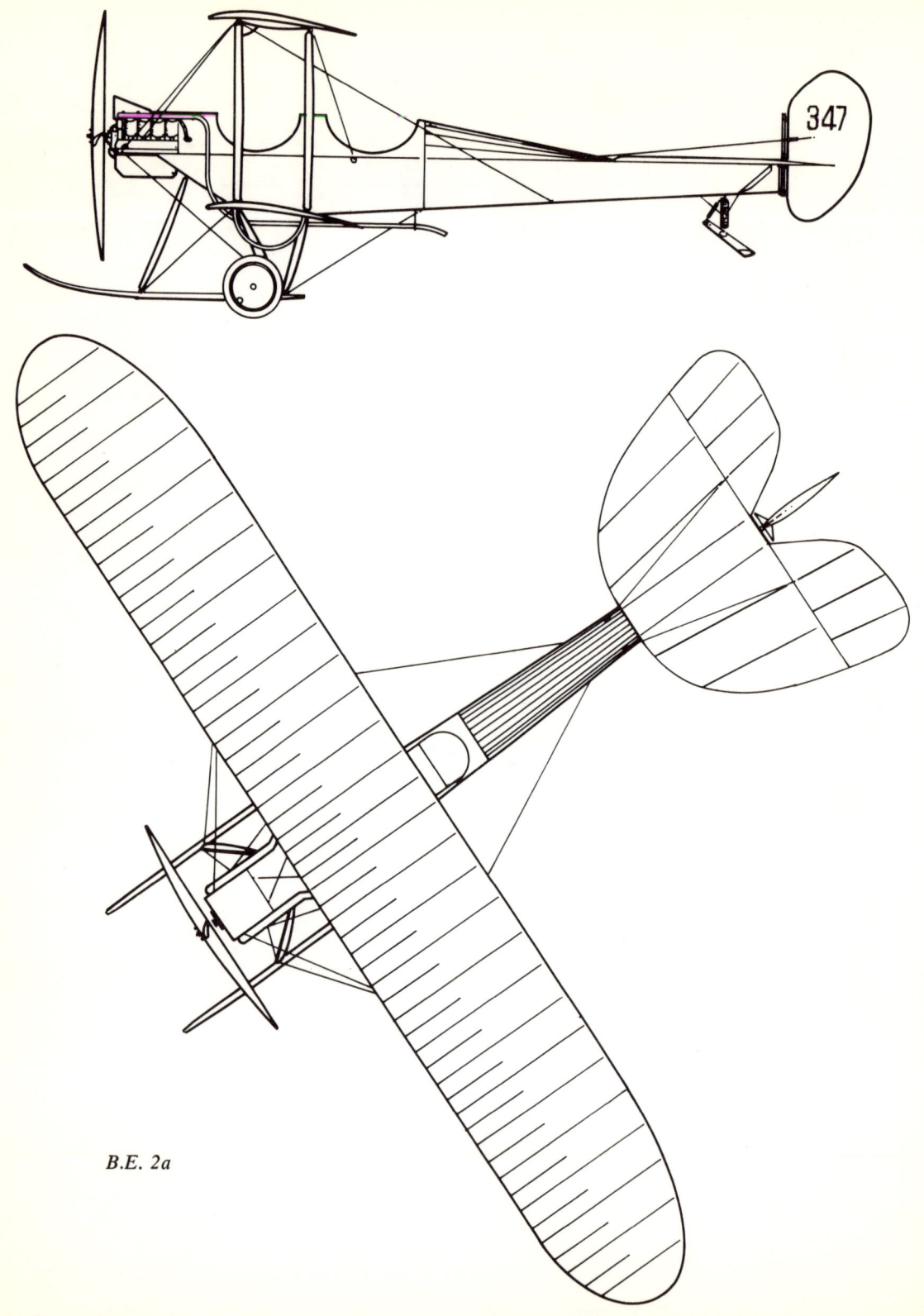

B.E. 2a

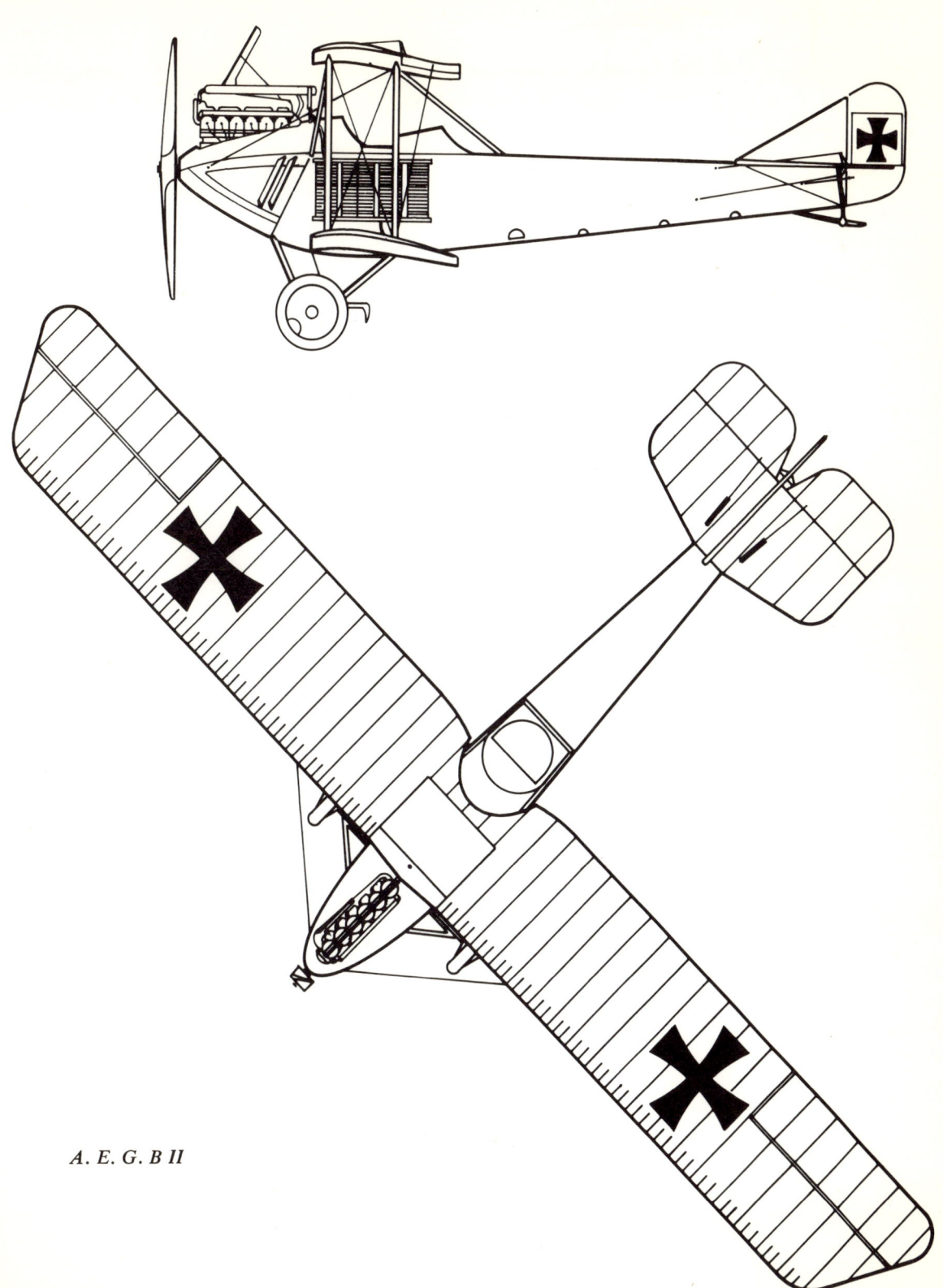

A. E. G. B II

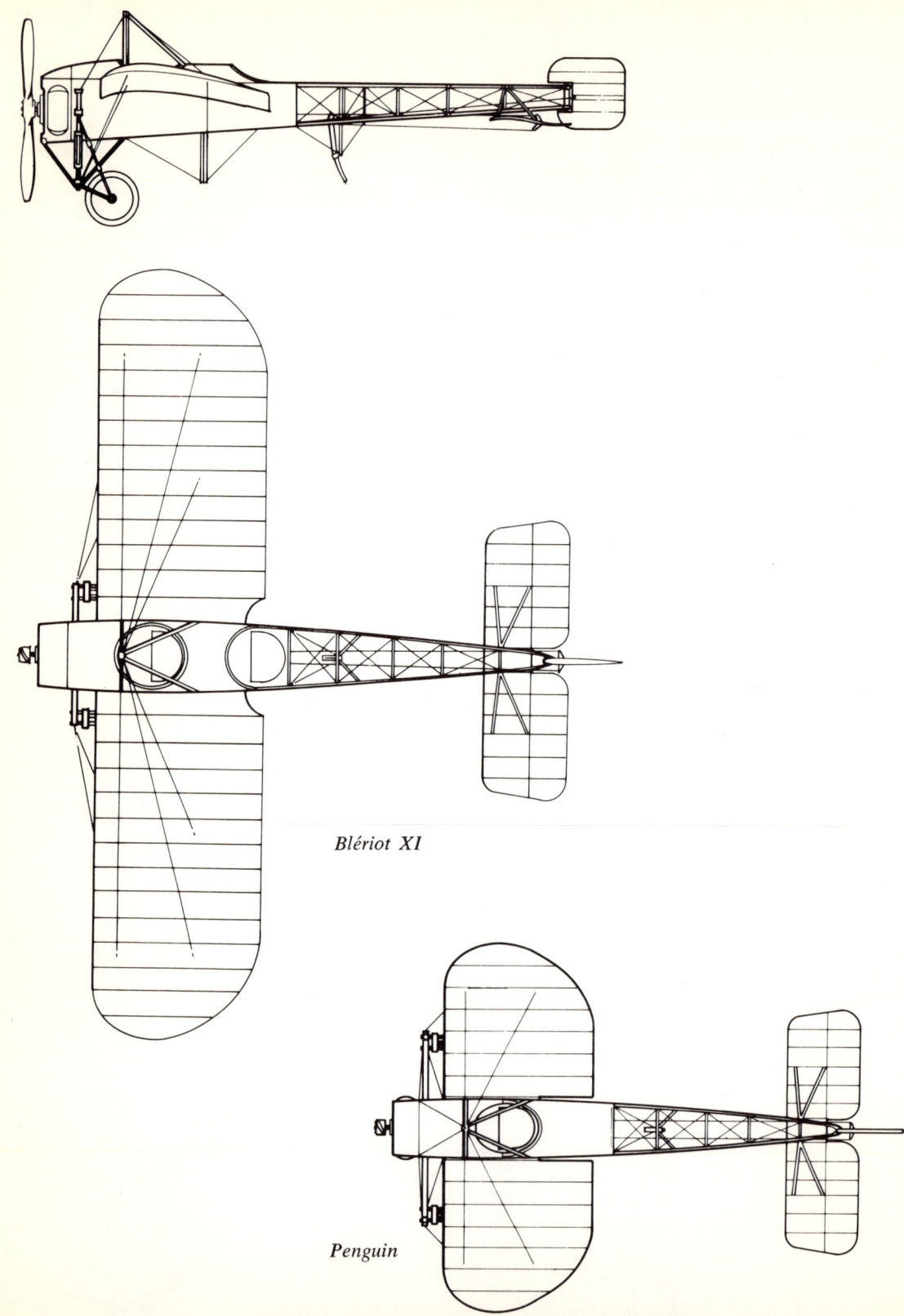

Blériot XI

Penguin

class, the *rouleurs,* or rollers. This class used regular Blériot monoplanes without clipped wings, powered by 60- to 80-horsepower rotary engines. The lessons of the *débutant* class were repeated and if the instructor was satisfied that the student had the machine under control, he was considered to be in the next class, the *décolleur,* or "unsticker." In this class the student was allowed to unstick himself from the ground. With his machine rolling straight across the field, tail up, he pulled back on the stick slightly and the machine rose in the air. His altitude was not to exceed three feet at first. Near the other end of the field, he cut the motor and the aeroplane settled back down to the ground. That's all there was to it. During the war the program was gradually speeded up, the students who looked fairly promising being passed through in a few days. Biddle went through all the courses thought necessary to train him as a combat pilot inside of five months.

His first forced landing was his first real test as a pilot. One day during a required endurance flight his motor conked out suddenly at an altitude of about 1500 feet. He had scarcely any time to pick out a good place to land, but nonetheless managed to get himself lined up with a narrow field bordered on one side by a stream. Because the stream had no discernible banks he concluded that the field was liable to be marshy, but mud is better than trees, so in he went. Holding the Blériot's tail low he glided in at near stalling speed. Just before touching down he pulled the stick back further so the tail would hit first. The aeroplane mushed down, the tail settled into the tall grass and mud and water sprayed in all directions. The machine stayed right side up, rolling only about fifteen feet before it came to a stop.

Biddle climbed out and walked around the dripping aeroplane to make sure that nothing was broken, then, with the help of some French peasants who happened by, he pushed it to dryer ground. There he changed the spark plugs from his emergency kit and instructed one of the men how to spin the prop without decapitating himself. With this help he got the motor started again, took off and returned safely to his base.

The authorities probably want these little emergencies to crop up, Biddle reflected, just to see how a man takes care of himself.

ADOLPHE PÉGOUD was born on 13 June 1889, at Monferrat (Isère), France. In 1907 at the age of eighteen he enlisted in the Fifth Regiment of the *Chasseurs d'Afrique,* a light cavalry outfit, then passed to the Hussars and ended up in a regiment of colonial artillery. While stationed at Toulon with the artillery, he made the acquaintance of *Capitaine* (Captain) Carlin, a military aviator, who gave Pégoud his first ride in an aeroplane. Pégoud summed up the experience in one word—joy. Under the aegis of Carlin he was detached to the aviation service as an assistant mechanic and was able to ride regularly with him. On his own, Carlin taught Pégoud how to fly. Discharged from the service in February 1913 Pégoud was uncertain what career to follow. He unsuccessfully offered his services to Serbia and Rumania, where some soldiers of fortune had reputedly done well as aviators, and finally landed a job as third-string test pilot with Louis Blériot.

He test-flew factory aeroplanes for a few months and in August 1913 got a chance to do something that promised a bit of celebrity—he was to demonstrate a parachute, the invention of a Monsieur Bonnet.

The parachute was of the familiar silk canopy construction, but, instead of being worn in a pack on the back, it was stowed in a canvas container attached to the outside of the aeroplane, behind the cockpit.

Pégoud took off in a Blériot monoplane and climbed to about 350 feet. He unfastened his safety belt and stood up, pulling the rip cord as he did so. The parachute snapped open, actuated by springs, caught the air and yanked him out of the cockpit. As he swung gently beneath the parachute, Pégoud was followed by a crowd of spectators. He landed in a tree, climbed down leaving his parachute draped over the branches, and was hoisted on the shoulders of the crowd. The aeroplane dived to the ground not far from the aerodrome and was wrecked.

It is worthy to note that successful parachute jumps were being made over a year before the war began. The reluctance of military commanders to encourage the intensive development and universal use of such life-saving equipment provides a very serious indictment indeed. Until 1917 the only parachutes regularly issued in the aerial services were those issued to the balloon observers and to some bomber crews. Through 1917 and 1918 German fighter pilots were regularly issued parachutes—such famous Ger-

Musée de l'Air / Paris

Pégoud.

man aces as Ernst Udet and Eduard *Ritter* von Schleich both escaped burning aeroplanes in parachutes—but it was not until after the war that parachutes became standard equipment for the fighter pilots of the Allied nations. The Allies lost some very valuable men as a result. Of all the rationalizations made by Allied brass to justify errors of judgment, the one which purports to explain why it was a "bad" idea to issue parachutes to fighter pilots was one of the most unfeeling and unreal. It was considered that to issue parachutes to fighter pilots would undermine their fighting spirit; the pilot who knew he had a chance to bail out would not, it was felt, go into a fight with the same "do or die" determination as one who knew the issue in any air fight must unalterably be kill or be killed. The pilots themselves appear to have been of the opinion that the security of a dependable parachute

Musée de l'Air / Paris

Pégoud and his mechanic.

might make it feasible to take a chance once in a while. Yet many fighter pilots were reckless youths who could be expected to put up a fight under any conditions, and it can be shown that many of them who had parachutes refused to wear them for fear of being thought cowardly. There is nevertheless no question that while the general use of parachutes would not have altered significantly the final outcome of the air war, such use would have preserved many lives to the ultimate great benefit of aviation. The whole issue is an excellent and dramatic example of the coarse texture of one kind of military mind and of the inadequacy of military methods to deal humanely with human problems.

The next experiment Pégoud wanted to perform was upside-down flying. He had been thinking about it for a time, but he had never heard of its having been done before. He contrived to have a machine slung up inside the hangar, himself strapped in, and then rolled over to simulate the upside-down flying attitude. When his ears turned red, the mechanics rolled him back. Satisfied that he had the feel of it, he went out and *did* it. He never stopped until he had tried everything. He never claimed to be a scientist, but he wanted to learn everything there was to learn about flying and the only way to do that was to experiment. He had an intuition that never failed him but no illusion that he was indestructible. "If I kill myself," he said, "so what? One less aviator. But if I succeed, how many valuable lives may be saved for aviation."

He went on tour, flying in air shows from Norway to Italy. The Paris newspapers hailed him as a hero. In September 1913 at Brooklands aerodrome a few miles southwest of London, he finished up his performance by flying past the stands with both arms raised above his head.

He was in Hamburg, Germany, preparing to embark with three crated aeroplanes for a tour of America, when the threat of war made it imperative for him to return to France immediately.

*   *   *

JOHANNISTHAL AERODROME was located in the suburb of Berlin from which it took its name. Some of the great firms of German aviation maintained their factories and showrooms there and gave flying lessons as a side line. In the autumn of 1913 Pégoud gave an exhibition of stunt flying at Johannisthal unlike anything the crowds had ever seen, and there to witness the exhibition was a young man of Dutch parentage and citizenship named Anthony Herman Gerard Fokker. Operator of one of the flying schools at Johannisthal, Fokker also owned a small factory at Schwerin in Mecklenburg which employed some fifty hands turning out a series of sport aeroplanes.

Fokker watched Pégoud's performance critically. He was good, all right, and the crowds loved him. Fokker decided he should do the same thing, only he would do his stunting in one of his own aeroplanes as an advertisement for his factory and his flying school. Fokker was a truly great pilot, but the aeroplanes he had thus far produced were just not good enough. About this time, however, his designer left him and Fokker's assistant, a twenty-two-year-old native of Cologne named Martin Kreutzer, inherited the position. Kreutzer was a competent designer and Fokker had a strong flair for judging the qualities of an aeroplane so the two of them worked well together, although Fokker himself was certainly no designer. They immediately began work on a new monoplane which was to be powered by the 80-horsepower Gnôme rotary engine. In layout the new machine somewhat resembled the Blériot, powered by the Gnôme, flown by Pégoud. It also somewhat resembled a second-hand French Morane that Fokker had pur-

Tony Fokker and friends.

Imperial War Museum / London

chased, but to the construction of the M.5, as the machine was called, Kreutzer and Fokker brought a major innovation: the fuselage and wing skeletons were built of welded steel tubing instead of wood. It was characteristic of Fokker to borrow ideas—in this case the form of the M.5 was inspired by the French machines—but it was also characteristic of him to want to do things better than the competition. In the new monoplane Fokker looped and stunted about Germany, thrilling spectators and, on one occasion, making a strong impression on General von Falkenhayn, the Prussian Minister of War, who saw him in the spring of 1914.

The last days of peace were played away; the time was fast approaching when the expensive toy, the aeroplane, like everything else that has ever been invented, was to be put to the uses of war.

*   *   *

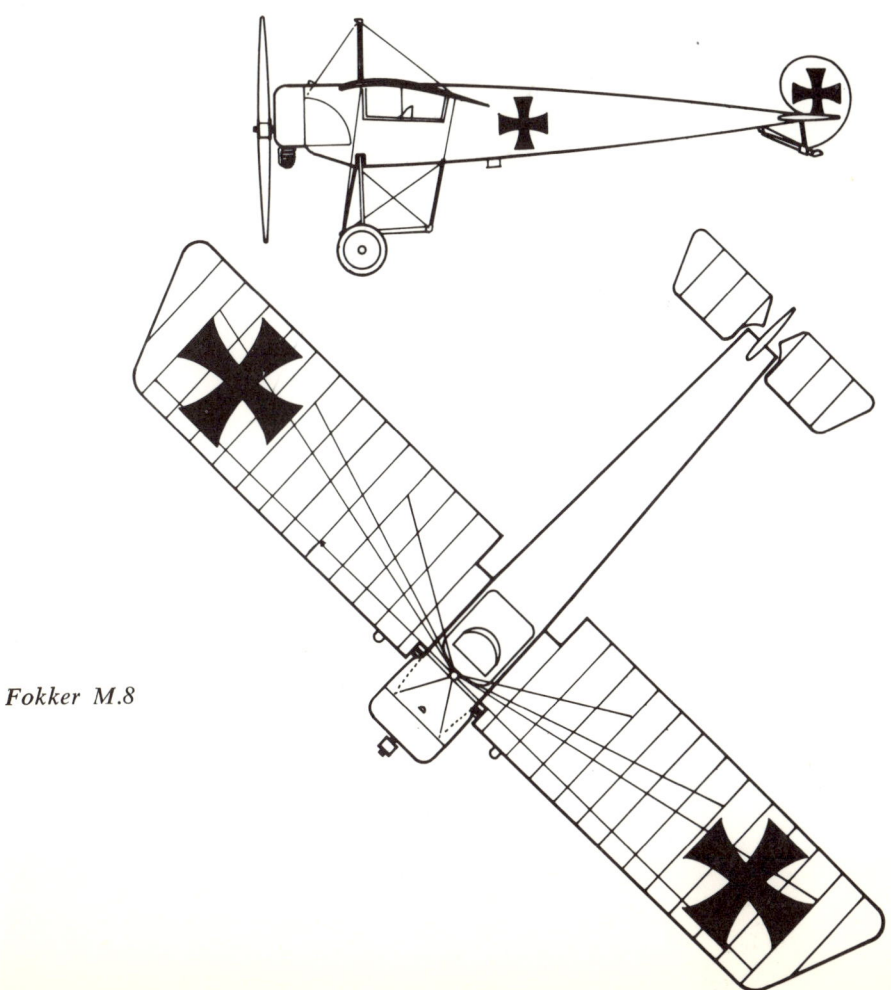

Fokker M.8

2 / "IT WAS TRAGIC..."

2

GABRIEL VOISIN, of the Voisin Aeroplane Company, started building aeroplanes with Blériot before the war. In 1907 he and his brother Charles established their own company, and although Charles was killed in 1912 the business carried on, so that by the time of the outbreak of the war, Gabriel was one of the major constructors in France. He regularly produced machines under military contract and began expanding rapidly like almost every other industry under the war economy.

In the French *Service d'Aéronautique* there had been a consistent effort from the beginning to organize squadrons—*escadrilles*—on a homogeneous basis, that is, to have them composed entirely of one make and type of aeroplane. The British Royal Flying Corps, on the other hand, was a mishmash of everything that came along. In the half-dozen squadrons in service when the war began, not one was uniformly equipped with a single type and some had as many as four or five. This made servicing and repairs a supply officer's nightmare. In organization, the Germans stood somewhere between the two extremes.

A few weeks after the outbreak of war, Gabriel Voisin approached *Capitaine* André Faure, the commanding officer of *Escadrille* V. 24 (Voisin Squadron No. 24), and suggested to him that all his aeroplanes should be armed. At that time aeroplanes were not armed at all, unless the observer of a two-seater felt inclined to take along a carbine or an automatic pistol on reconnaissance missions. Even so, weapons were more often taken up for the purpose of self-defense in the event of a forced landing than for fighting in the air. In the British Royal Flying Corps, the R.F.C., it was officially discouraged for airmen to take up machine guns because the commanders, who never lost their faith in the horse, believed the extra weight of the gun would seriously affect aeroplane performance.

To Voisin and Faure, however, if to no one else, it was clear that one aeroplane armed with a machine gun could shoot another aeroplane down. The Voisin was a pusher, with its engine in the back, so the passenger in the back seat had a clear field of fire ahead of him. Voisin designed a simple tubular mounting to take a Hotchkiss machine gun and Faure had one such mounting installed in each of his aeroplanes. The apex of the mounting was over the pilot's head and the passenger in the back seat stood up to shoot. Voisin obtained the guns—he visited the Hotchkiss armory himself and talked them out of twelve guns.

During the first two months of the war Allied and German pilots met many times in the air over the battlefields—the front had not stabilized as yet. A few aviators had taken a shot on one side or the other, but in the vast majority of cases when enemy aeroplanes met their crews simply waved and went about their business. War in the air and the age of air-fighting were inaugurated on 5 October 1914, in the sky near Rheims by two men of V. 24, Joseph Frantz, a pre-war pilot, and his mechanic-observer-gunner, Louis Quénault.

Joseph Frantz won his military pilot's ticket in January 1911. At the military concourse at Rheims in the same year he piloted a Savary biplane,

Voisin L2

Voisin L2

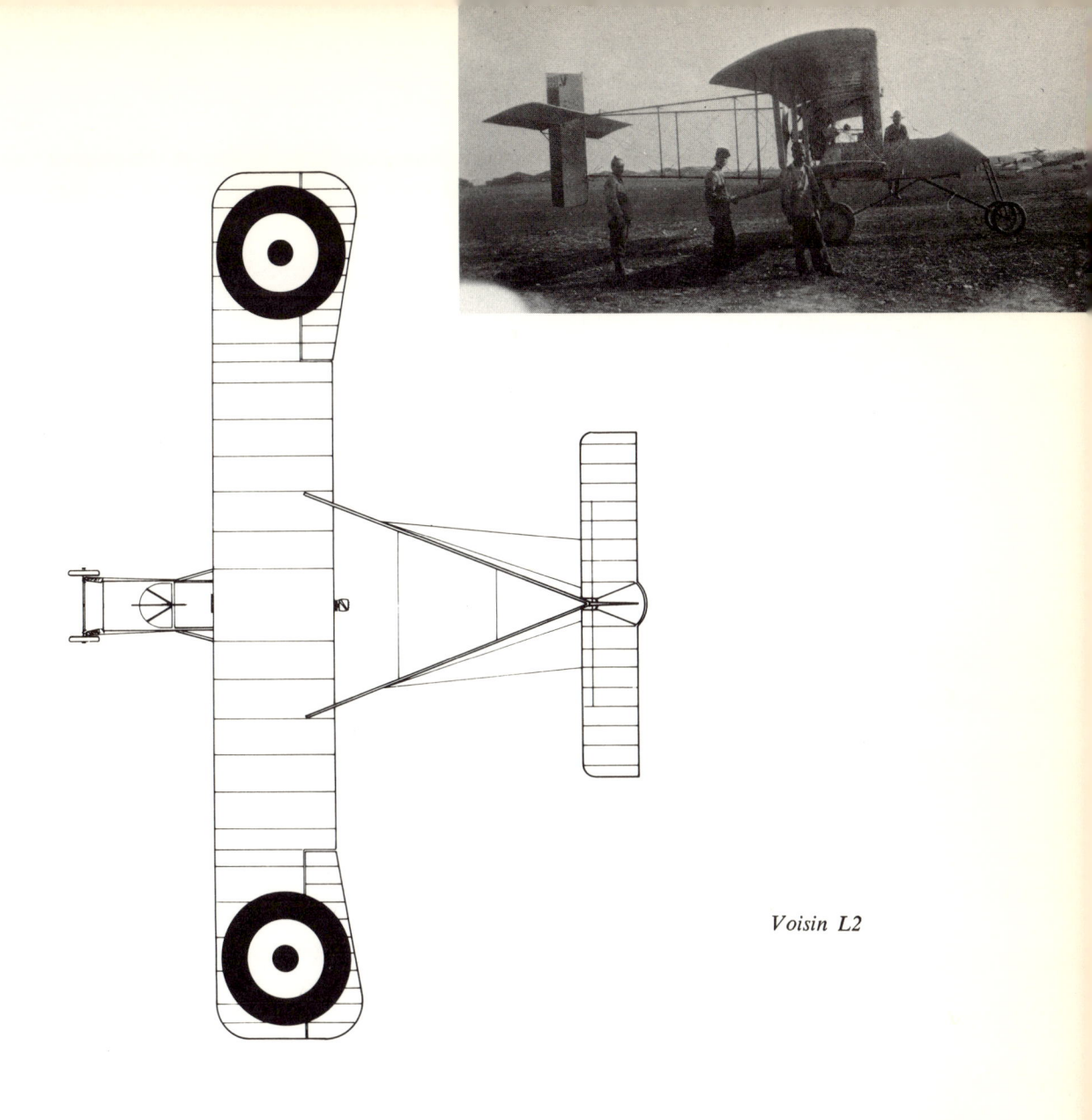

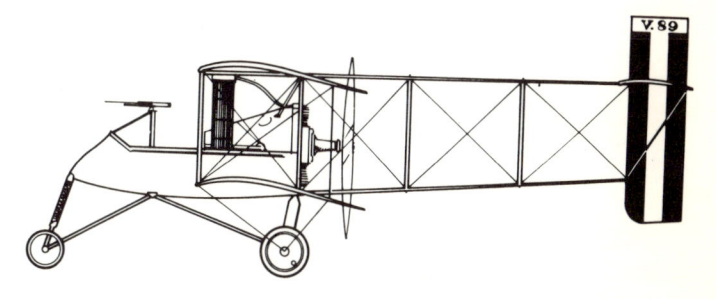

Aviatik B

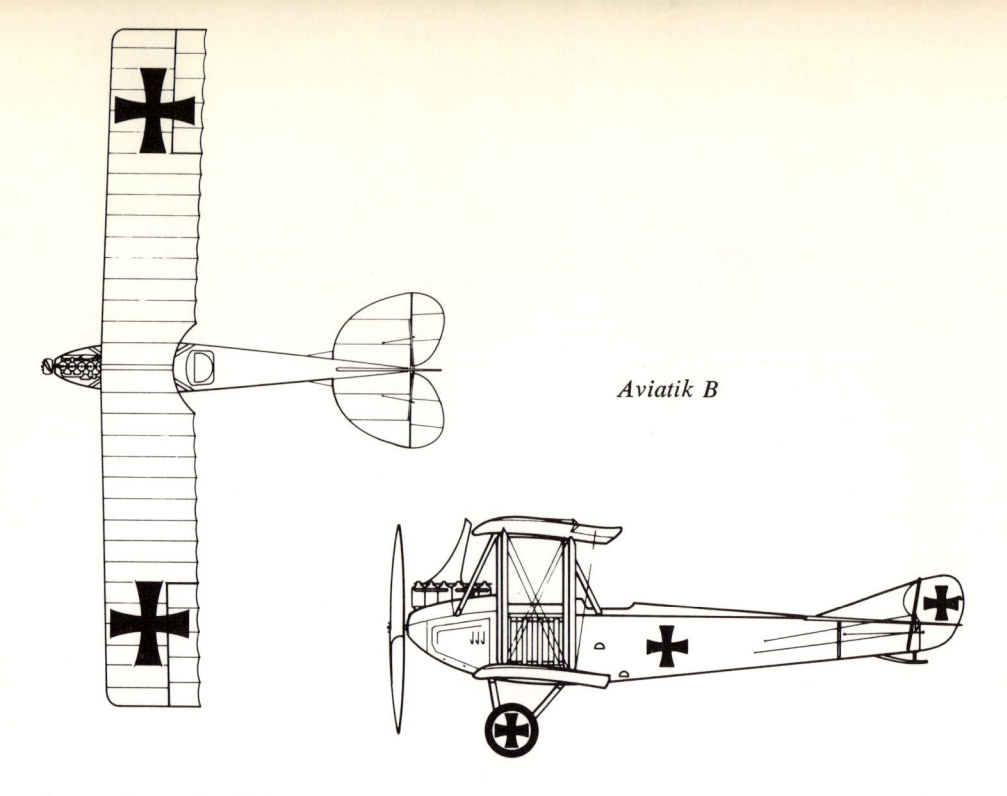

the engine of which was produced by the firm of Labor-Aviation, and a company mechanic was sent along to attend to the servicing of the engine: this was Louis Quénault. The two formed a team for the duration of the service trials and when Frantz on the outbreak of war joined V. 24, then in the process of being formed, it was arranged for Quénault to join the same squadron as his mechanic.

On 5 October *Capitaine* Faure ordered them on a mission to the neighborhood of Rheims. The squadron was at that time bearing the designation VB. 24, the "B" indicating that it was chiefly occupied with bombing duties. The "bombs" that Quénault was to drop on the target that day, an enemy troop concentration, were six 90-millimetre artillery shells, and he was to drop them by hand.

Returning from their mission Frantz spotted an Aviatik two-seater, Quénault stood up to man the gun, and the first air fight in history took place. In his own words, Frantz described the subsequent events: "I immediately dived to cut off the retreat of the Aviatik and maneuvered to place myself behind the enemy. That done, we had approached to a point where we could

Sergeant Frantz and Corporal Quénault. Photo taken at the time of their victory as they posed under the tail of the Voisin they flew on that occasion.

Musée de l'Air / Paris

clearly distinguish the movements of the pilot and his passenger. At this moment the passenger shouldered a repeating carbine and opened fire at our machine. Quénault then opened fire, shooting straight ahead over my head.

"The Hotchkiss, well steadied by the tripod, was easy enough to maneuver, but was subject to stoppages when fired fully automatic. We had therefore decided to shoot one round at a time. Quénault fired one by one forty-seven rounds—at the forty-eighth the gun jammed. Quénault, whose composure was astounding, commenced to strip the receiver to clear the jam when the German machine lurched before our eyes, began to dive, then turned on its back and smashed into the ground in a cloud of black smoke."

Witnesses on the ground who had followed the fight, ran to where the aeroplane had gone down. It had crashed in a wood beside a small pond and the motor was almost buried in the marshy ground. Pieces of wreckage lay scattered about. It was found that the pilot had been killed by Quénault's fire and the aeroplane had then fallen out of control, bearing the observer to his death.

RAYMOND SAULNIER of the aviation firm of Morane-Saulnier, at Villacoublay near Paris, wrote a letter in May 1914 to the Inspector-General for Air outlining his idea for a single-seater fighter. The letter went unanswered and apparently failed to evoke a flicker of interest in the War Office. Saulnier himself lost interest in his original idea until the shooting started.

One of the best pre-war aeroplanes was the Morane-Saulnier N monoplane. The Morane machines, as they were called, were a racy-looking family and the N was no exception. With a top speed of one hundred miles per hour and the ability to climb to 10,000 feet in twelve minutes flat, it was also a racy performer. Saulnier's idea was to fix a Hotchkiss to the aeroplane within reach of the pilot so he could reload it and clear it when it jammed. The rapid maneuverability of the N monoplane suggested to him that the gun should be mounted rigidly and aimed by aiming the whole aeroplane. The logical direction of fire was straight ahead and that is where he ran into problems, for there was at the beginning of the war no way to shoot through the propeller. He tried synchronizing the rate of fire of the machine gun with the rate of revolutions of the propeller, but soon found that the engine speed could not be controlled precisely enough—the engine was bound to speed up or slow down with the result that the gun shot holes in the propeller. He then tried armoring the propeller, and at this point Roland Garros took over.

A well-known pre-war aviator, Garros had won a number of honors for the Morane-Saulnier company. In December 1912 he established a world altitude record and in September 1913 had become the first man to fly across the Mediterranean Sea. He was a wealthy, polished man of the world, a piano virtuoso and an exhibition pilot of superlative skill. When the war began he offered his services to the *Service d'Aéronautique* and was assigned to a Morane squadron, *Escadrille* M-S 23, commanded by *Capitaine* Vergnette. When Raymond Saulnier wrote to him about his idea for an armed single-seater, Garros immediately applied for permission to report to Villacoublay and work on the project with him. He arrived in November 1914 and by January 1915 had developed a primitive but workable "deflector gear." The technique was simplicity itself: a machine gun was bolted to the fuselage of the aeroplane directly ahead of the cockpit, butt end projecting

Imperial War Museum / London

Morane-Saulnier "N"

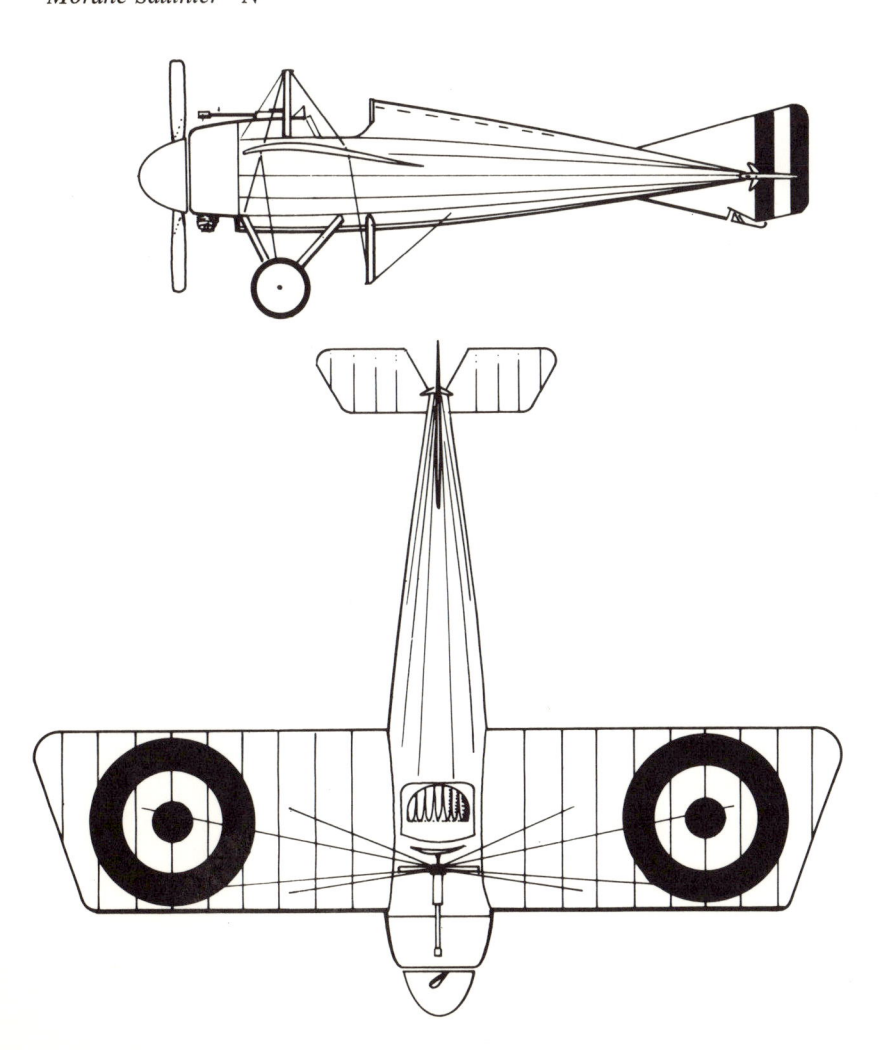

Musée de l'Air / Paris

Roland Garros.

into the cockpit within easy reach of the pilot. Directly in front of the muzzle of the gun, which fired straight ahead, steel wedges were affixed to the rear of the propeller blades. The wedges presented their points to the gun and so deflected any bullets that struck the propeller.

In February of 1915 Garros reported back to M-S 23 from Villacoublay with his armed single-seater. For several weeks he flew on the usual variety of missions that were assigned before the days of specialization—reconnaissance, observation, photography and the like—and never got a crack at an enemy aeroplane. The sky is a big place and it would be a mistake to suppose pilots met enemy machines every time they went up.

On the first day of April Garros took off alone with two hundred pounds of bombs to drop on the railroad station at Ostend. At a point several miles on the other side of the lines he caught sight of a German two-seater that was flying more or less directly over the French lines and drawing the fire of the French anti-aircraft batteries. The enemy machine, an Aviatik, was some 1500 feet above him so Garros immediately began to climb to put himself on the same level. Since he was in a position to cut off the retreat of the Aviatik, Garros allowed himself a considerable length of time—six or eight minutes—to maneuver into position. Judging himself to be well placed he rushed straight in. At a range of about one hundred feet he fired. The observer in the two-seater answered with a rifle. Garros fired off the twenty-five round Hotchkiss clip and quickly reloaded, firing off another clip. The Aviatik dived away, but Garros clung to its tail. As the two machines descended to perhaps 3000 feet, Garros closed up and triggered a very short burst from his third clip. The Aviatik suddenly caught fire. An immense flame enveloped it and it fell spinning toward the earth.

"It was tragic, frightful," wrote Garros. "At the end of perhaps twenty-five seconds (which seemed long) of falling, the machine dashed into the ground in a great cloud of smoke."

In his own words the episode ends on a note of shocked horror: "I went by car to see the wreck; those first on the scene had pilfered souvenirs—side arms, insignia, and the like. I took energetic steps to retrieve them. The two corpses were in a horrible state—naked and bloody! The observer had been shot through the head. The pilot was too horribly mutilated to be examined. The remains of the aeroplane were pierced everywhere with bullet holes. . . ."

*   *   *

INSEPARABLE as boys, twins Jean and Pierre Navarre went separate ways in the army. Born 8 August 1895, they were both interested in aeroplanes, but only Jean chose the *Service d' Aéronautique*; Pierre went into the *Génie*, or Army Engineers.

Jean won his pilot's certificate in September 1914 and was sent to *Escadrille* MF 8, equipped with Maurice Farman machines. He was flying alone the first time he saw an enemy aeroplane. The German was alone too and he flew up alongside Navarre and waved. Navarre waved back, then grabbed his carbine and threw a shot at the other man. The German pilot dived away. Navarre was unable to follow because his aeroplane almost stalled out when he let go of the controls to shoulder the carbine. He leveled off and continued on his way, but by the time he returned to the field he had decided he was through with Farmans. They were no good for fighting— what he wanted was to fly in a Morane squadron, and he immediately applied for a transfer.

After some impatient waiting he got his transfer and was posted to *Escadrille* M-S 12 at Muizon near Rheims. The squadron was commanded by *Capitaine* de Bernis, and flew Morane-Saulnier *Parasols* on photography and reconnaissance missions. The *Parasol* was so named because the single wing, supported above the fuselage by struts, shaded the front seat like a parasol. By April 1915 Navarre had two confirmed victories and was the champion of the French infantry in the sector, for he never failed to put on an exhibition of stunting over the trenches.

Morane-Saulnier Parasol

Jean Navarre. Note the good luck charm.

Musée de l'Air / Paris

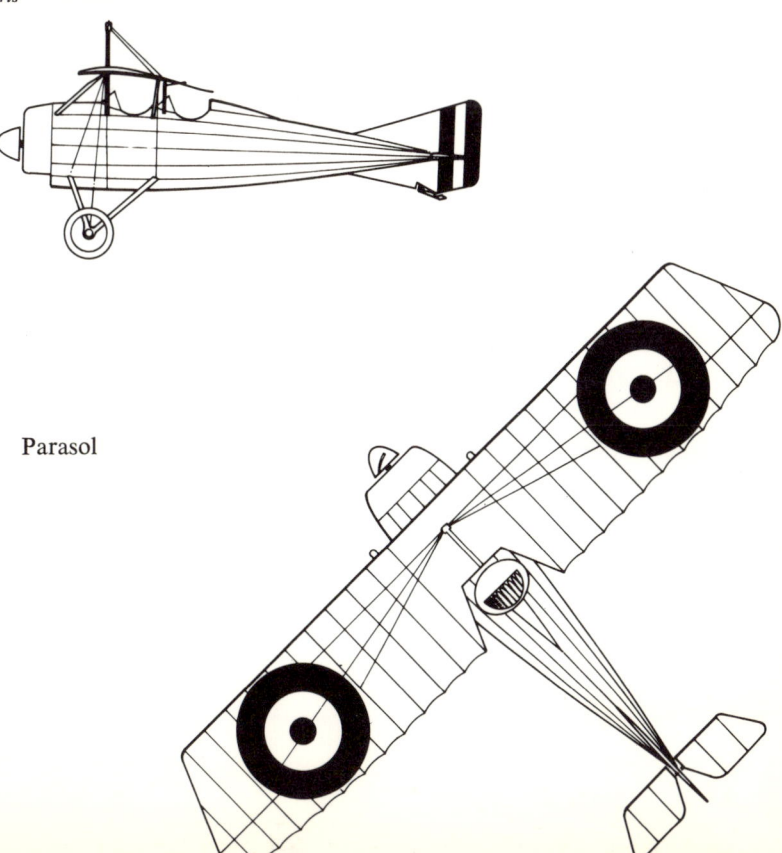

Parasol

One day Navarre and an observer named Girard spotted another *Parasol* mixing it up with two German machines. They joined in the scrap, Girard standing up in the front seat to fire a hand-held Hotchkiss machine gun over the wing while Navarre banged away with a pistol. The nearer machine was hit and its motor sputtered to a stop. Its pilot tried to dive away. Even with a dead engine he might have made it to the German lines for he built up a fair turn of speed in the dive, but he pulled out too low over the French lines and the troops opened up with a fusillade that brought him down for keeps. The other one got away.

Now their own engine was acting up, vibrating badly, and Navarre and Girard were forced to set down as quickly as possible. Safely down, they looked over their aeroplane and found that they had almost shot themselves down, for Girard in his excitement had put a couple of holes through the propeller.

*   *   *

AS A LEADER, an innovator and an inspiration to his men, one of the great aviators of the war was a Saxon named Oswald Boelcke. He was born in Giebichenstein near Halle on 9 May 1891, and gained his army commission by way of the Prussian Cadet Corps. He first witnessed military aviation before the war while on maneuvers; his interest aroused, he applied for flying training. He was accepted and sent to the Halberstadt Flying School, where he obtained his pilot's certificate two weeks after the outbreak of the war, on 15 August 1914.

In September Boelcke reported to a squadron on active service in the field, one in which his brother Wilhelm, a Regular Army officer, was serving as an observer. For the next few months the brothers flew regularly as a team, Oswald as the chauffeur.

The squadron in which the brothers flew was one of thirty German and four Bavarian units of which the German air service's field strength was composed. The equipment for each squadron was six machines, uniformly biplane two-seaters with 100-horsepower motors. They were regularly issued without armament. The squadrons were ancillary to the usual Army Corps service units and were called simply Flying Sections—*Fliegerabteilungen*. These six-machine *Fliegerabteilungen* were under the command of an *In-*

spekteur or Director at Corps level, and were completely subservient to Army Corps commanders. Their work was reconnaissance, observation, artillery-spotting, photography and liaison. The latter was simple. It consisted chiefly of shooting pre-arranged signal flares or dropping messages so that ground units could more or less keep in touch with one another.

Heinz J. Nowarra

Boelcke.

For the first year of the war all the air services had the same jobs, worked out on maneuvers before the war, and no improvisation was allowed.

Reconnaissance flights were those whose object was to spy out new developments on the other side of the line; observation and photography were methods of keeping those developments under surveillance. Spotting for artillery meant signalling battery commanders, either visually or by wireless, exactly where their shots were falling. It meant circling one spot for an hour or so, bored and frightened to death, keeping a watch on the shooting and reporting every shot so the gunners would know if they were putting them over or short, and waiting for the antiaircraft guns to blow them to bits. It was the dullest, most dangerous work in the air.

After the war had gone on long enough for everyone to realize it was not going to be over "by Christmas" because Christmas was already past, the air services began expanding. In April 1915 Oswald Boelcke was selected, because of his experience, to help shape up a new Flying Section, *Fliegerabteilung 62 (Fl. Abt. 62),* and get it operational. Boelcke had been awarded the Iron Cross First Class in February 1915 for having completed fifty observation missions, which was very nearly a record.

The standard aeroplanes in the German air service, up to the spring of 1915, were two-seater biplanes of the B class with 100-horsepower motors. These machines had proved their value for photography and observation, but were unable to defend themselves. French gunners in handy machines such as the Morane-Saulnier *Parasol* created a serious problem for the Germans, forcing the development of the C class. This was basically the same as the B class, but there were three significant improvements: the horsepower was upped to one hundred fifty, the pilot and observer traded seats and the observer was equipped with a Parabellum machine gun. The pilot, now in the front seat, enjoyed an improved view and the observer, now in the rear seat, had some room to swing his Parabellum about.

Taking advantage of this new arrangement, Boelcke, in the summer of 1915, managed to bring off his first successful air attack. With an observer, *Leutnant* (Second Lieutenant) von Wuehlisch, he attacked a Morane *Parasol* near Liétard. Boelcke made the first pass and after considerable maneuvering worked himself into a good position for von Wuehlisch to put a burst into the French machine. The *Parasol* heeled over and fell into a wooded area. Boelcke and von Wuehlisch didn't know it at the time, but their victim fell into a wood that was part of the estate of the Count de Beauvricourt; the observer in the *Parasol* had been the Count himself.

*   *   *

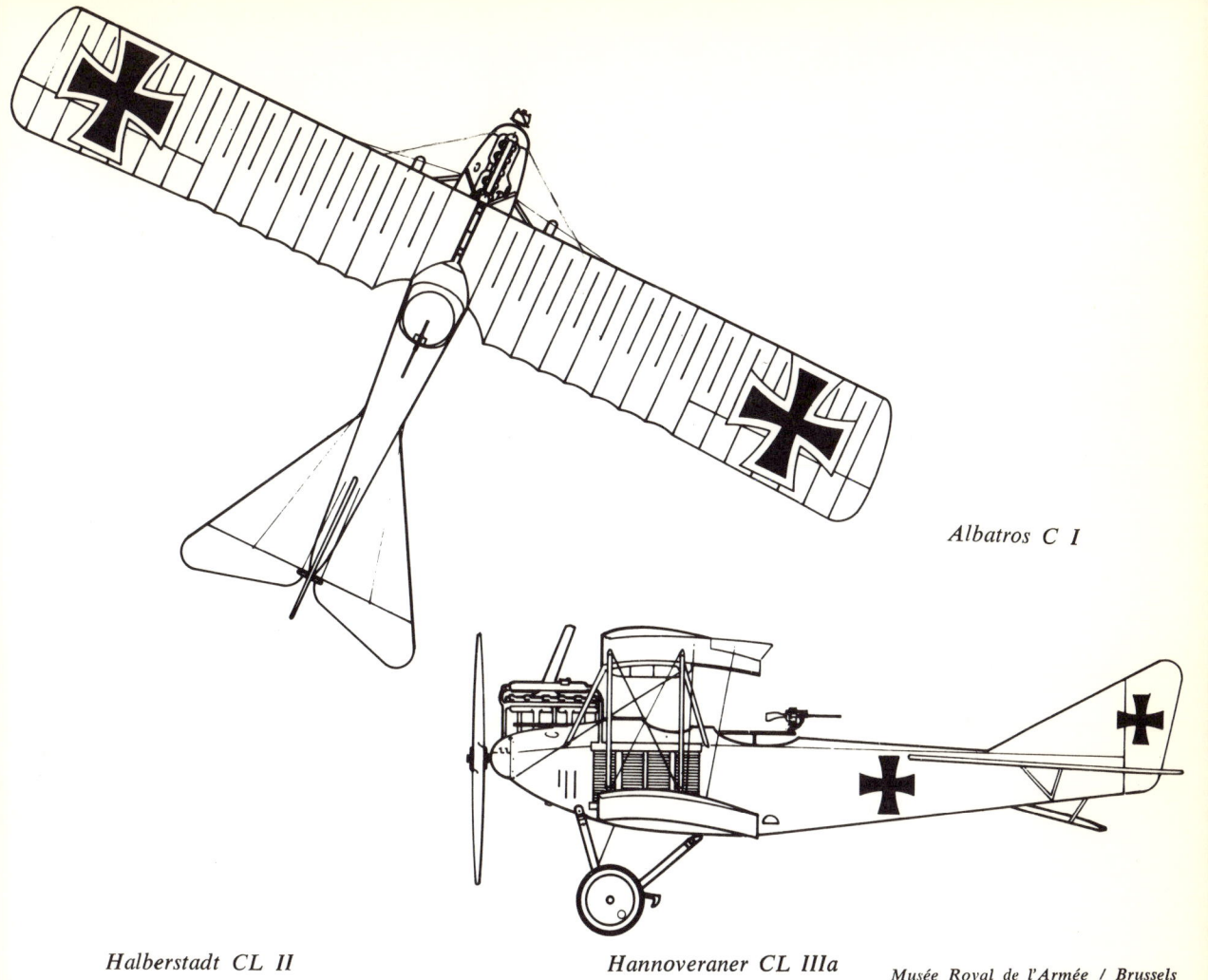

Albatros C I

Halberstadt CL II Hannoveraner CL IIIa *Musée Royal de l'Armée / Brussels*

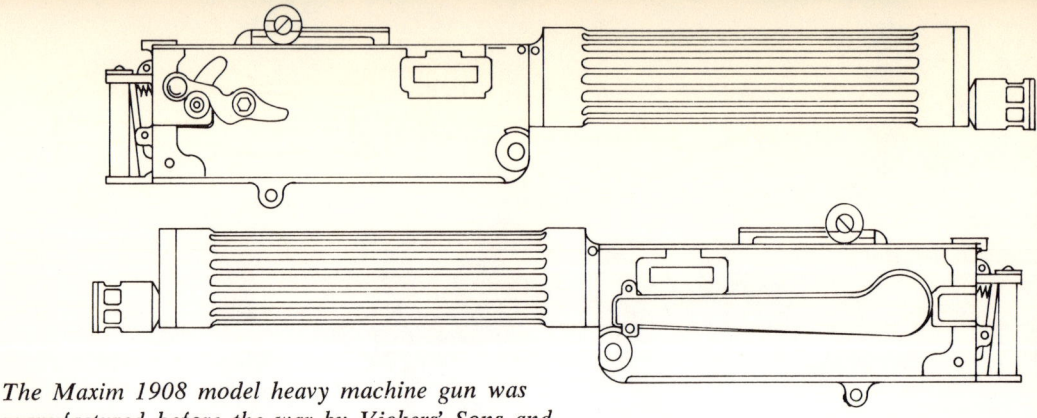

The Maxim 1908 model heavy machine gun was manufactured before the war by Vickers' Sons and Maxim, Ltd., of London and Knightsbridge. The Vickers company started making Maxim guns for the British government in 1888. During the war vast numbers of "Vickers guns" as they were called were produced for all the Allied air services.

1908 Maxim/Vickers Heavy Model

The 1908 heavy Maxim was also the basic weapon of the German air services. Before the war the Prussian state arsenal at Spandau, Berlin, began manufacturing the gun under license for the German army. A modification of the basic design in 1915 led the Germans to label the gun the 08/15 model. The Allies called this gun a "Spandau" gun after the arsenal where it was produced, but it was really a Maxim gun just as the Vickers was.

The Germans developed a light model called a Parabellum for aerial gunners.

The 1908 heavy Maxim was a water-cooled weapon in its infantry forms. In the air it was adequately cooled by the rush of the slip stream alone, and the water jacket, retained merely to support the barrel, was fretted or fluted to permit cooling air to flow freely around the barrel. The Parabellum version sometimes dispensed with the jacket. For the benefit of fighter pilots special cocking levers were developed which gave increased leverage to help in clearing jams.

In 1916 a double drum was developed that held 97 rounds. A light aluminum casing was attached to the gun covering the barrel and the gas cylinder. This casing, sometimes called a radiator, was intended to cool, support, and protect the barrel, but was ultimately dispensed with as it was found that the barrel did not need the support and the slip stream effectively cooled the naked barrel.

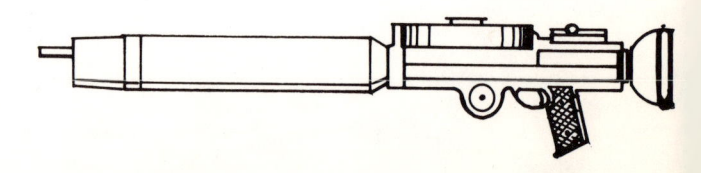

1916 Lewis Machine Gun with radiator

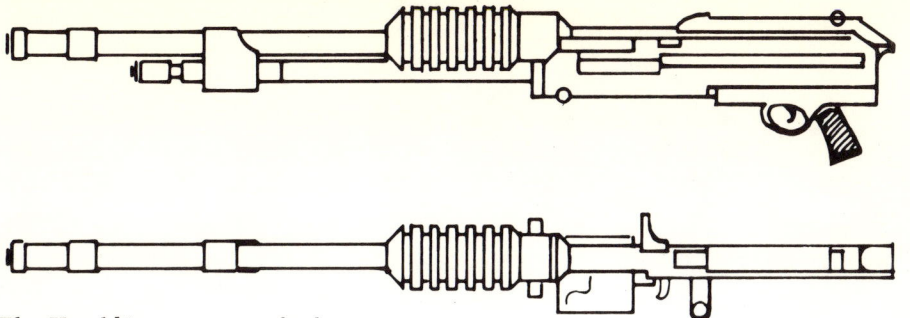

The Hotchkiss was a standard automatic rifle type of weapon in the French and Belgian armies at the outbreak of the war. It was an air-cooled clip-fed weapon. The clip was a rigid, spring-loaded magazine of 25 rounds capacity.

1885 Hotchkiss Machine Gun

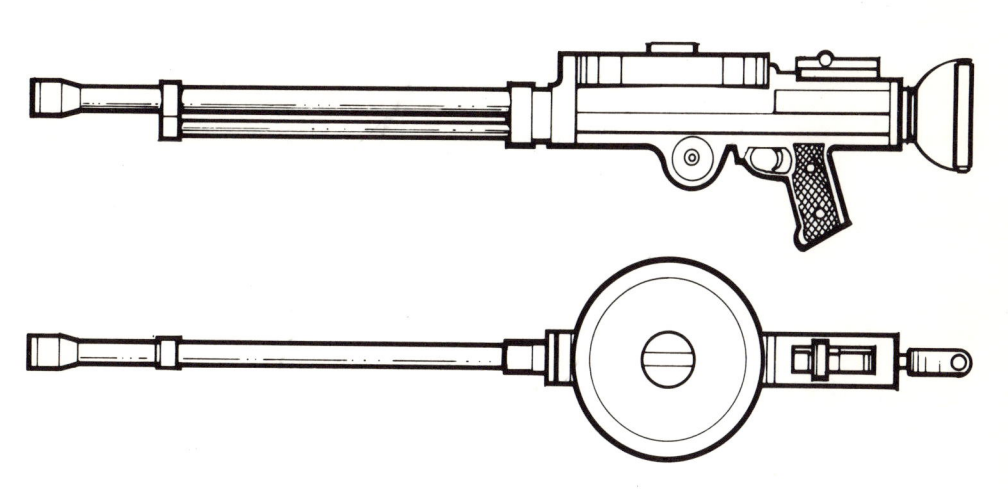

The 1911 model Lewis gun was an air-cooled weapon fed by spring action from a revolving drum containing 47 rounds. It was the standard light machine gun of the Belgian and British infantries. Because of its light weight it was selected as the weapon with which to arm aerial gunners.

1911 Lewis Machine Gun

Musée de l'Air / Paris

Fonck in Caudron G4. Note the unconventional mounting of the Lewis gun.

British R.E. 8

Musée Royal de l'Armée / Brussels

A Spad 7 being armed for combat.

Fokker M.5

3 / BLUE MAX

3

ROLAND GARROS enjoyed a good run of luck while it lasted, but it lasted a very short time. Between the first of April 1915 when he introduced what can be called the first fighter and the eighteenth he shot down three German aeroplanes. Some writers say that he shot down five and was therefore the first "ace," but he only got three, and it was Pégoud who was called the first ace. Pégoud's run of luck lasted a little longer and he got six enemy machines.

On 18 April 1915, Roland Garros tried to bomb a train in the vicinity of Courtrai in Belgium. He dropped one bomb on the track and another nearby while German troops fired at him from the ground and from the train. His motor was hit during the shooting and he was forced down, taken prisoner and his aeroplane fell into the hands of the Germans.

A thorough report of this lucky capture was sent to the technical people at the military airfield at Döberitz, Berlin, followed by the propeller itself. When the Germans tried the prop on a test stand with one of their own motors and a Parabellum machine gun, they smashed the whole works. The French standard-issue machine gun ammunition used a relatively soft copper-coated bullet, whereas comparable German ammunition was jacketed with steel. Obviously, the deflector gear was not going to work for the Germans as it had for the French. Tony Fokker was therefore called in, chiefly because he was producing a single-seater similar to the Morane, the Fokker M.5, and the problem was explained to him. He was issued a Parabellum, given the remains of Garros' propeller and told to get to work.

Back at the shop, Fokker's engineers immediately saw that the only effective way to solve the problem was to shoot *between* the blades of the propeller and that armoring the propeller was unsatisfactory in every way. They decided that the simplest method would be to have the propeller itself trigger the gun by means of a mechanical linkage. The actual linkage connecting the prop and the gun was one of push-rods actuated by cams, and by replacing the propeller with a plywood disc which was rotated by hand, it was found that the system could be adjusted to close and efficient tolerances. When it was tried out in flight it worked smoothly and Fokker advised the armaments experts at Döberitz that he had a fighter ready to demonstrate. The new armament was accepted and several models of the M.5 with machine gun were delivered to various Flying Sections—the *Fliegerabteilungen*—for operational assessment. The M.5 was given a new designation, being now styled E I, the E indicating that it was an *Eindecker* or monoplane type.

Ehrhardt von Teubern

Boelcke and his Eindecker.

Imperial War Museum / London

Fokker E II

The Fokker *Eindeckers* were used in increasing numbers during the summer and fall of 1915 and many future German aces started their careers in them. The British and French two-seaters that were still coming over the lines for observation, photography and artillery-spotting were for the most part either alone or unarmed or both, and thus were easy prey for the *Eindeckers*. The situation grew so bad for the British that the R.F.C. called the last half of 1915 the period of the "Fokker Scourge."

Fokker E I Eindecker

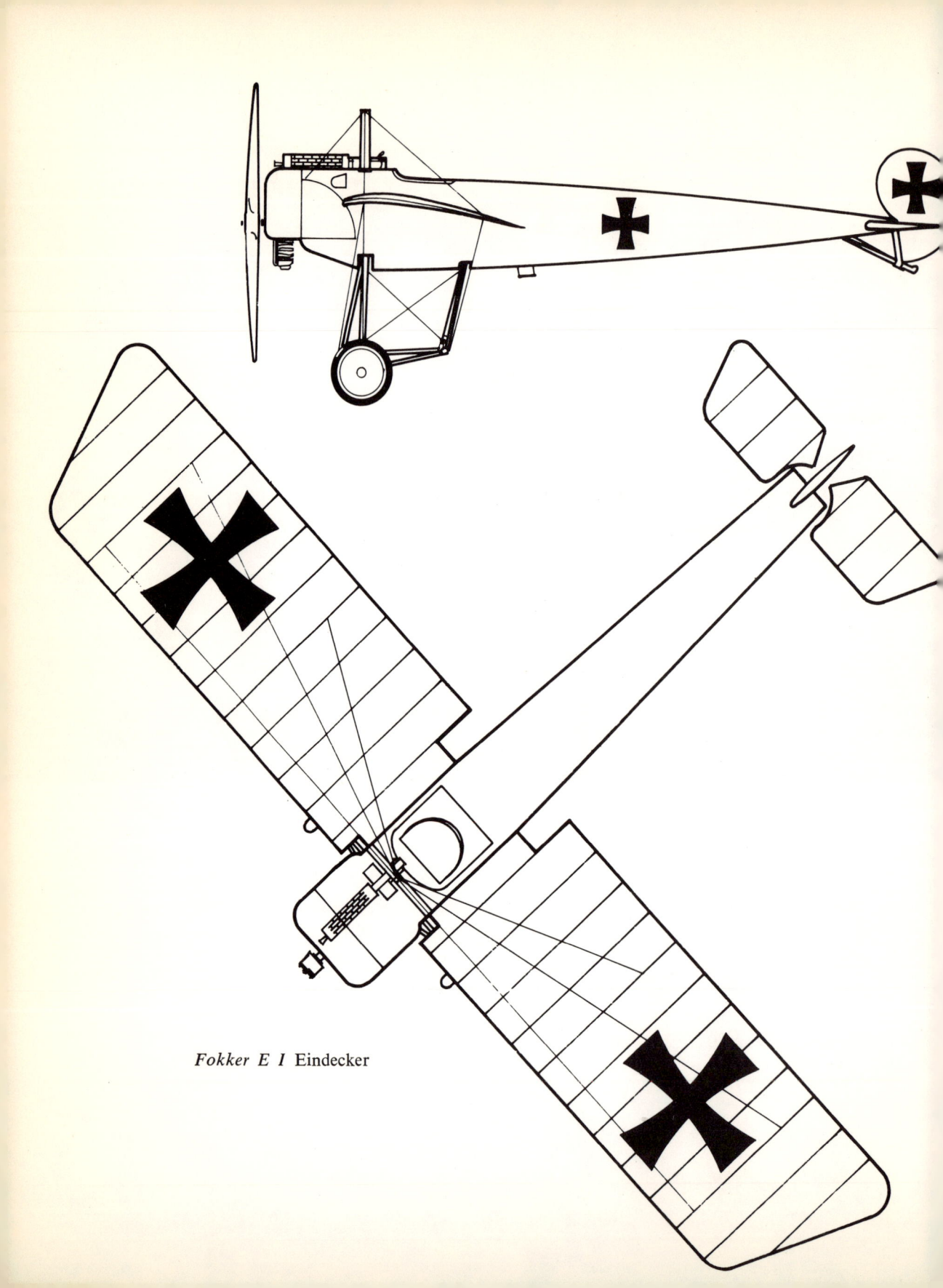

Pfalz E I

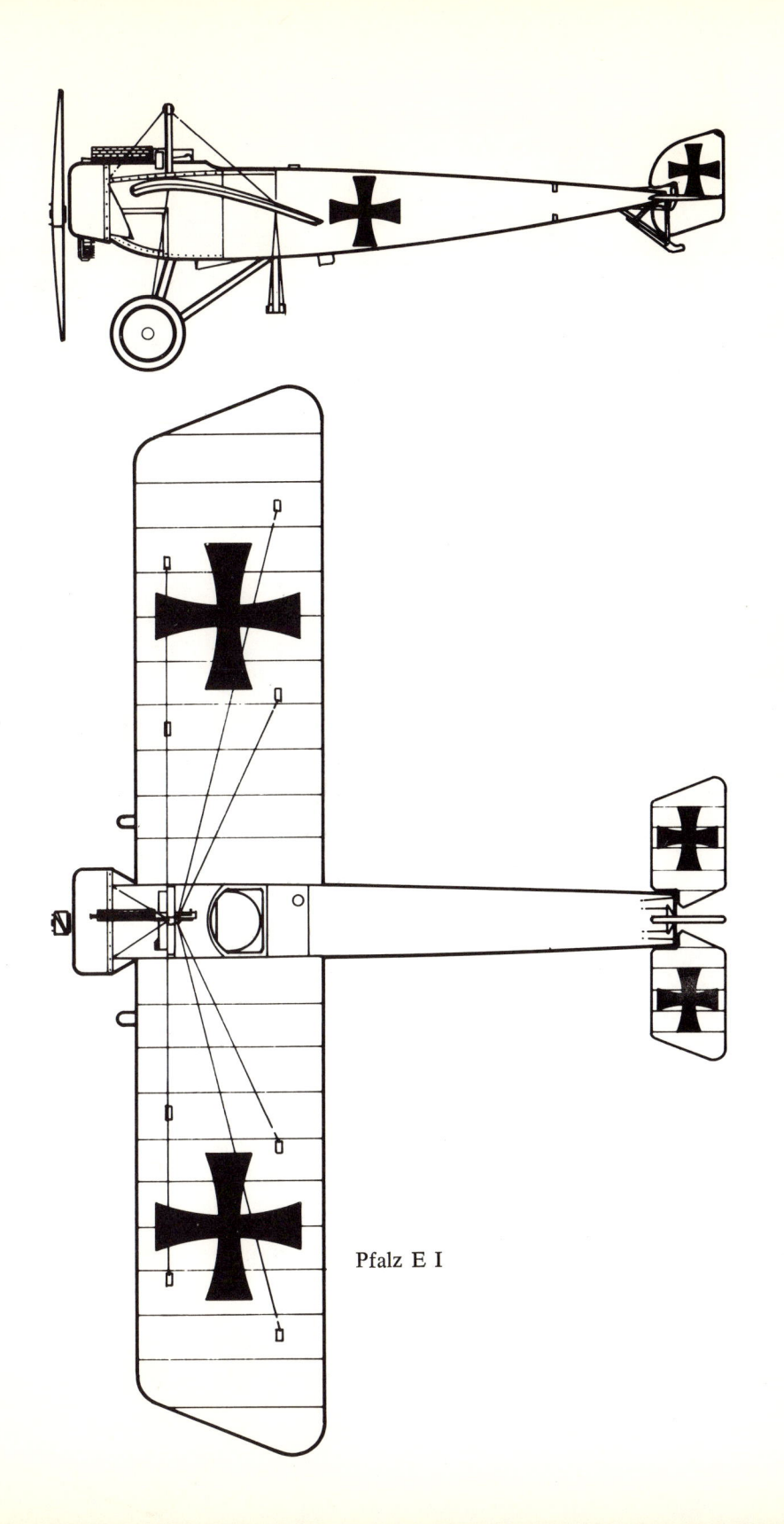

Erhardt von Teubern

Fliegerabteilung 62

Two *Eindeckers* were issued to *Fliegerabteilung 62*, both of them earmarked for Boelcke, although the first man in the squadron to go out hunting in one was the commanding officer, *Oberleutnant* (First Lieutenant) Kastner, and the first man to score a victory in one was *Leutnant* Max Immelmann. Immelmann was born in Dresden on 21 September 1890, and was graduated from the Royal Saxon Cadet Corps Academy there at Easter 1911. He resigned from the army to enter the Technical College in Dresden since he wanted to be an engineer, but on the general mobilization for war, he was recalled to his regiment. When he learned that his unit was not immediately scheduled for active service, he applied for aviation training. He was accepted for pilot training at the end of 1914, passed his flying tests in the early part of 1915 and was sent to *Fl. Abt. 62* in May. He held at that time the rank of *Fähnrich* (loosely, sub-lieutenant), his promotion to *Leutnant* coming through at the end of July. For the first few months that he was with *Fl. Abt. 62*, Immelmann was a two-seater pilot, a chauffeur for an observer. He persuaded Kastner and Boelcke to let him try his hand at the *Eindecker*. And with no more special instruction than what Boelcke passed on to him conversationally, he took one up and brought it down in one piece. Immelmann was a fine natural pilot, although he achieved nothing out of the ordinary in the two-seaters, and the light *Eindecker* was just the kind of machine he needed to feel at home in the air.

The growing success of the *Eindeckers* against the British two-seaters was a matter of concern to the R.F.C. and a major policy change soon came about. It was laid down as a hard and fast rule that any machine proceeding on a reconnaissance mission was to be accompanied by no fewer than three other aeroplanes suitably armed for defense. At the same time the British started a campaign against German aerodromes, hoping to cut off the problem at its source.

On the first day of August 1915, the R.F.C. bombed the aerodrome of *Fliegerabteilung 62* which was located near Douai in northern France. Boelcke took off in one *Eindecker* to give chase to the British; Max Immelmann took off in the other one. Boelcke caught up with the enemy machines, but was forced out of action on his first pass by a jammed machine gun. That left Immelmann alone. He followed the British machines for a while, then closed in on a straggler. He attacked this machine several times and fired off a hundred rounds before he saw it go abruptly into a steep glide. It landed in German territory and Immelmann landed close by it, jumped out of his *Eindecker* and ran up to the enemy aeroplane. The pilot was flying alone, having carried bombs instead of an observer, and he was wounded in the left arm. Immelmann shook his right hand and then saw his prisoner into the hands of a doctor.

Immelmann's first victory was clumsy and amateurish, but he and Boelcke were delighted, for not many pilots could claim a victory the first time they went up as fighters. Boelcke and Immelmann both became masters in a very short time and it can be said that they were among the founding fathers of the German fighter service.

Boelcke was the organizer, the man who could put across his ideas on air policy and who, ultimately, defined the role of the fighters in a series of conferences at Supreme Headquarters (*Oberste Heeresleitung,* or *O.H.L.*). Broadly speaking, the fighters have one purpose, to shoot down enemy aeroplanes, but this purpose achieves two functions: preventing enemy aeroplanes from completing their missions, and protecting friendly aeroplanes while they complete theirs. Boelcke was a quiet, unassuming man, possessed of dignity and the ability to inspire obedience. Immelmann was considerably more youthful in spirit and apparently without any outstanding qualities as a leader. He was one of the first pilots to achieve fame during his lifetime. He was best known to the British because he did all of his flying on their front. Boelcke moved around somewhat and his early victories were against the French. Immelmann's chief quality was perhaps his initiative—he appears to be one of the first of the early fighter pilots who tried to make use of aerobatics as tactics. The so-called "Immelmann turn," for example, was performed many times by Pégoud before the war. Other pilots included it in their exhibition flying. It was a half-loop with a roll-out at the top, the kind of graceful maneuver requiring smooth co-ordination that Pégoud loved. When Immelmann used it as part of his combat tactics, it became a method of attacking, changing direction and gaining height to attack again all in one maneuver.

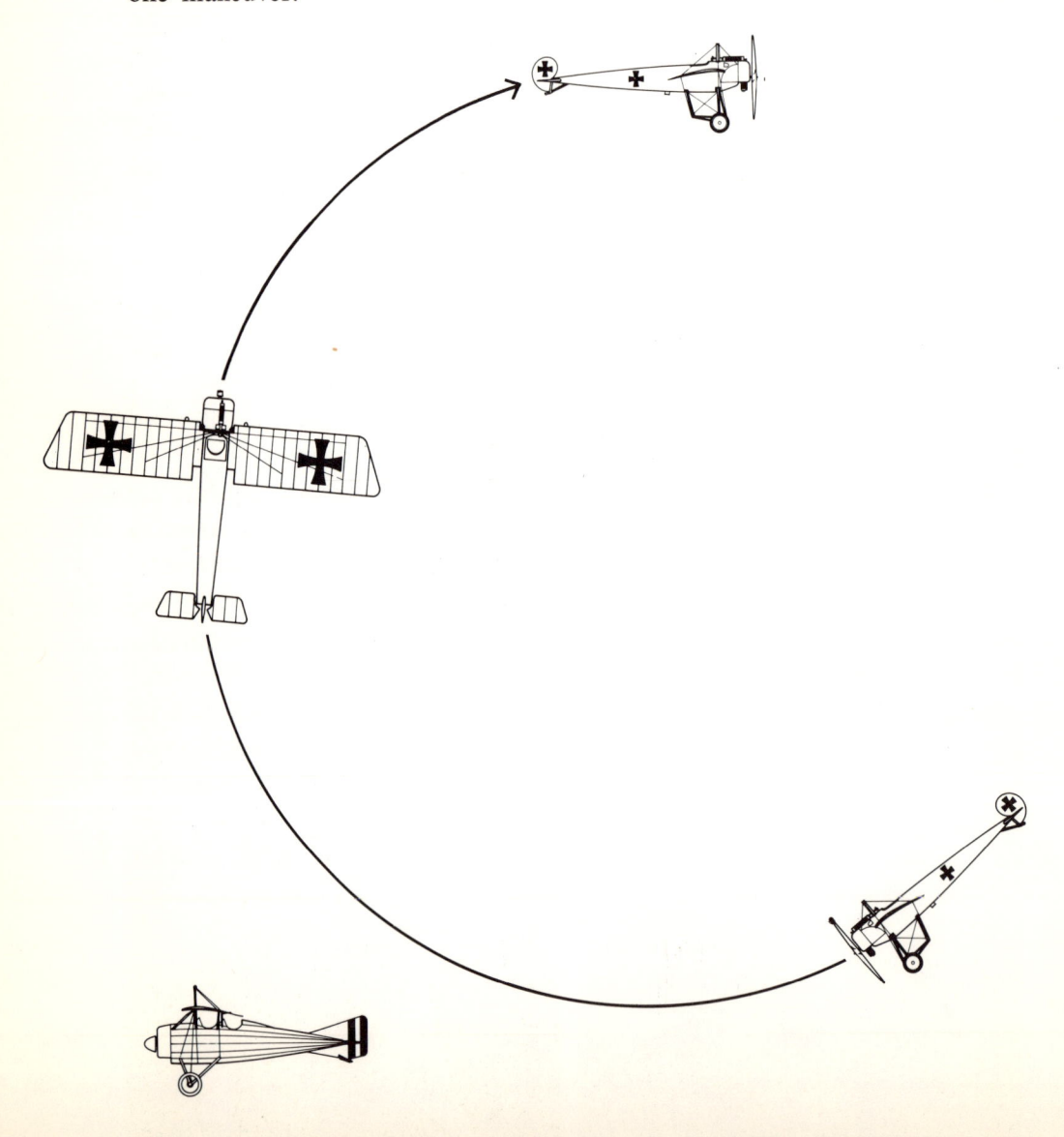

Immelmann and Boelcke, operating on different parts of the front, seemed to be in friendly competition. Their scores slowly rose until by January 1916 they had eight confirmed victories apiece. On 13 January they were both awarded the Order *Pour le Mérite,* the first aviators to be so honored. The medal itself was a gold-bordered blue-enameled cross, and was dubbed the "Blue Max" by the British after Max Immelmann. The Order itself— literally "for merit"—was Germany's highest award outside those reserved for the Imperial family, the nobility and generals. For the German aviators it was considered to be comparable to the French *Légion d'Honneur* or the Congressional Medal of Honor, and came to be the hallmark of an ace. Instituted by Frederick the Great, it bore a French name because French was always the language of European court etiquette.

In February 1916 Boelcke was promoted to *Oberleutnant.* During the spring of the year he shot down ten French aeroplanes at Verdun. In May he was promoted to *Hauptmann,* or Captain, and was one of the youngest men in the German army to hold the rank and wear the *Pour le Mérite* as well.

Immelmann.

Boelcke.

ADOLPHE PEGOUD was not long in making a name for himself as a war pilot. He was recalled to the artillery on the general mobilization, but as the greatest exhibition pilot in Europe he did not have long to wait before he was granted a transfer to the *Service d'Aéronautique*. At first he flew the usual army co-operation missions, reconnaissance, photography and the like, and was in the habit of carrying a good luck charm—a little plush penguin—with him in his Morane. Since the elementary training machines were called Penguins, his little doll was something of a personal joke.

In the spring of 1915 Pégoud was transferred to another Morane squadron, *Escadrille* M-S 49, stationed at Fontaine near the southernmost part of the front, down by the Swiss border. There he flew an armored-propeller Morane similar to the one Garros had introduced on 1 April, and scored several victories with it. About this time the French began to put a new aeroplane into service; Pégoud was one of the first to fly it. It was called the Nieuport *Bébé,* and it has with justification been called the first modern fighter. The Nieuport company was founded by Edouard de Niéport in 1910, survived him when he was killed in 1911, and in 1914 acquired the services of a naval engineer named Gustave Delage as chief of the design staff. The *Bébé,* or Baby, was far superior to the *Eindecker* in speed, climb, ceiling, and maneuverability, and only lacked a heavyweight machine gun like the Parabellum to outclass it in every respect. The *Bébé* went into service without an interrupter gear, its single Lewis gun being fixed to the top wing to fire over the propeller.

Three Bébé Nieuports lined up at aerodrome.

Nieuport Bébé

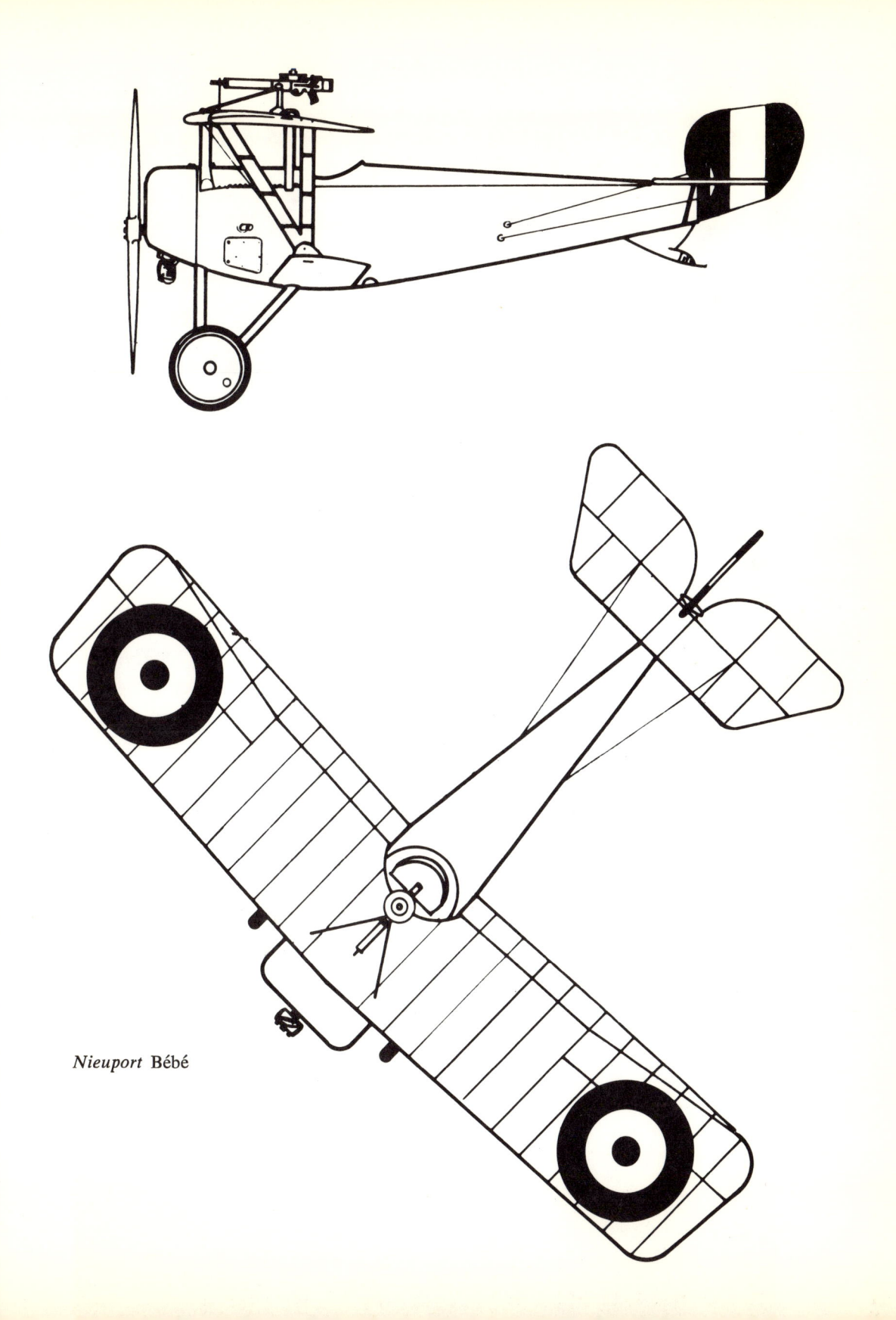

Closeup of Bébé Nieuport.

In July 1915 Pégoud downed a two-seater while flying the Morane. He wrote a brief account of the encounter in his diary: "An Aviatik is sighted. . . . Soon distinguish superb Aviatik. Try to draw it into our lines. Several feint attacks. Won't come, flies along front. Seeing this, dive on him and immediately pass under him while he shoots at me with machine gun located in rear. Shooting not accurate, his own fuselage in the way. Try to keep myself directly under him. Succeed with quick maneuvers, following movements of enemy aeroplane exactly. Zoom up to within one hundred fifty feet, start firing with first clip of twenty-five cartridges, aiming a little behind motor. . . . After ten rounds *Boche* nosedives, flames come out of fuselage. . . ." Pégoud watched the enemy machine go into the ground, then turned and headed for home.

Because Pégoud was so well known for his pre-war achievements, the handful of victories that he won (six) in a time when aerial victories were virtually unknown received considerable publicity in the press. When his score stood at five, the newspapers started calling him an *as,* or ace. The expression *as* was current sports slang in France; it derived from the name of the high card in a deck of cards and was taken to mean champion. Pégoud was the *as* of the day; a drink was named after him, and a brand of cigarettes, and five became the fortuitous standard by which one qualified as an ace.

At 8:30 in the morning of 31 August 1915, a telephone call from the front-line infantry came to the aerodrome requesting that someone go up and chase away a German two-seater that had been spotted snooping around. Pégoud, who was in the habit of standing by ready for such interceptions, quickly took off in his *Bébé,* found the German machine and traded a few long bursts with its gunner. He banked away to reload, then drove in again from the side and a little above. One bullet from the German gunner's Parabellum went through his heart. From 10,000 feet the *Bébé* dived straight into the ground.

Squadron mates, who arrived at the site of the crash by auto, found four gendarmes and a number of soldiers of the 117th Territorial Regiment, standing in a silent circle on guard over the wreck. The body of the first ace was covered by a strip of fabric from a wing. Still recognizable was Pégoud's good luck charm which his friends took back with them—the penguin.

ERNST UDET was born in Munich in 1896 and was interested in aeroplanes from the time he was a very small boy. Some of his adventures, such as jumping off the porch roof with an umbrella, are part and parcel of the early folklore of aviation—boys were trying such stunts from Moscow to Los Angeles. In 1941 when he was a general in the German *Luftwaffe,* bitter disillusionment drove him to commit suicide. It was a sorry end for one of the most successful fighter pilots of the 1914–1918 war.

Udet first served as a motorcycle dispatch rider and applied for aviation training at the end of 1914. He was at first turned down on the grounds that he was too young, so he talked his father into paying for civilian flying instruction at the Otto Flying School in Munich. On completion of the school he applied again for admission to the air service and was accepted.

The first squadron with which Udet flew operationally was *Fliegerabteilung 206,* stationed at Heiligenkreuz near Colmar in Alsace. His regular observer was *Leutnant* Bruno Justinus, their aeroplane was an Aviatik and the work was mostly artillery-spotting.

They very narrowly escaped a crash in September 1915 when a bracing wire for the outer end of the right wing snapped. Without the wire to steady it, the wing tip flexed in the wind, the left wing went down and the machine went into a steep sideslip. Udet wrenched the stick over to level the aeroplane and throttled back at the same time, but was unable to recover complete control. Justinus, realizing that unless the aeroplane were leveled off it would continue to slip right into the ground, climbed out of his seat and worked his way out on to the wing so that his weight would bring the right wing down. Udet gaped at him as he sat nonchalantly with his arms and legs wrapped around the struts. He shouted to him to come back, so Justinus returned to his seat, kicked out the plywood panel that separated the two cockpits and brought his own muscle to bear on the stick. The aeroplane

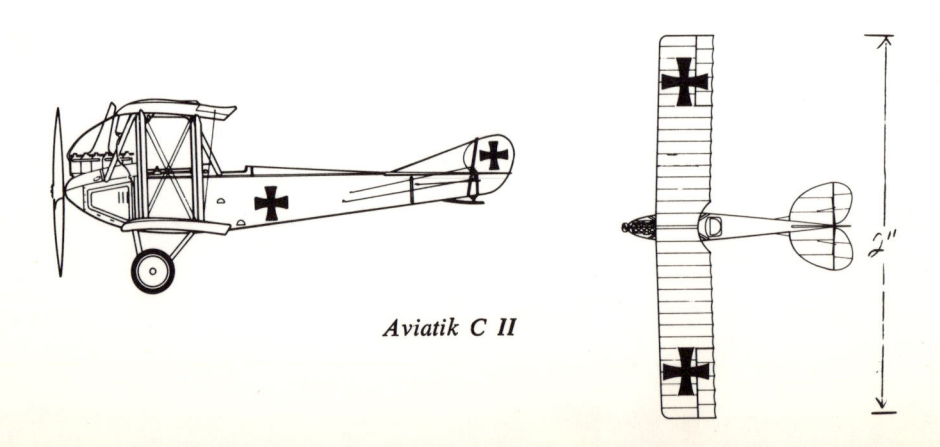

Aviatik C II

Udet.

Imperial War Museum / London

slowly righted itself. With power cut back the aeroplane steadily lost height, but with the two of them on the stick they managed to keep it level and land safely in an open field. The same day two other men of the squadron crashed and were killed, possibly as a result of the same kind of accident. Udet and Justinus were awarded the Iron Cross for having saved their aeroplane, but as Udet later said, they were quite satisfied to have saved their necks.

Udet applied several times for a transfer to a unit where he might have a chance to fly an *Eindecker* and finally made it late in 1915. His first victory came in March 1916 when he shot down a French Farman that was taking part in a bombing raid. Udet was alone and there were about forty aeroplanes in the French formation, but he managed to bring off one good attack by climbing above the enemy and diving right through them. He heard bullets from the French gunners hitting his machine as he opened fire in his dive. He saw a stream of white smoke suddenly pour from the engine of his victim and then he was through the formation. He continued his dive to put distance between himself and the French gunners. As he leveled off a thousand feet below, he saw the Farman he had hit, now flaming, tumble down. One of its crew had fallen out, and, with arms and legs outstretched, was slowly turning over and over.

* * *

U.S. Air Force

4 / STORKS

4

ORGANIZED FIGHTER AVIATION began during the long and drawn-out battle of Verdun which the Germans opened on the night of 21 February 1916, with a colossal artillery barrage. The one thousand two hundred twenty heavy guns massed for the curtain-raiser represented the largest concentration of firepower in history. For the next several months, from February to June, the earth was mauled along a short fifteen-mile front until it looked like the barren face of the moon. The landscape still bears the scars of the battle fifty years later.

At the very start of the battle the Germans held air superiority and their photography and artillery-spotting aeroplanes flew over the French positions free from interference. With their opening barrages they wrecked French aerodromes, and the *Eindeckers* completed the job by driving the French observation machines from the sky. The sight of German aeroplanes continually hovering overhead was very bad for French morale, and the actual work they accomplished co-operating with the artillery was worse.

General Henri Phillipe Pétain took command of the defense of Verdun within a few days of the start of the battle and in one of his first orders stated the absolute necessity of the French taking air superiority away from the Germans. Another new man then appeared on the scene, Colonel Barès, Chief of Aviation at French Army Headquarters (*Grand Quartier Général*, or *G.Q.G.*). Barès left *G.Q.G.* to come to Verdun personally to supervise the rebuilding of French air strength. He brought in new units to raise the establishment from four to sixteen *escadrilles*. The fighter establishment was particularly strong, being raised from one to six *escadrilles*. He also brought in some good men to organize the new groups, among whom the most spectacular personality was *Commandant* (Major) Tricornot de Rose, who took charge of all the fighters.

Tricornot de Rose, former air chief for the Fifth Army, held the first military pilot's certificate ever issued in the French army. A Dragoon and a professional soldier, he transferred to the *Service d'Aéronautique* in 1910, qualifying as a pilot in March 1911. In August 1914, at the beginning of the war, he was flying a long-distance reconnaissance when dry tanks forced him to land on the highway near a frontier village. He obtained gasoline

Musée de l'Air / Paris

de Rose.

in the village and was filling his tank when a spearhead of German cavalry came marching down the road at the other end of the village. Impassive, de Rose topped off his tank, started his motor and took off over the heads of the startled enemy troopers. He was an experienced, resourceful officer, a skilled pilot and was known far and wide for his magnificent walrus moustache.

The Nieuport *Bébé* was available now in sufficient numbers to form complete *escadrilles* of twelve aeroplanes, and de Rose laid down the first doctrines of offensive formation flying. He ruled that the fighters were to fly in formations of three to six machines and that their mission was to seek and destroy enemy aeroplanes wherever they could be found.

Shortly after the start of the battle of Verdun the Germans, believing that their two-seaters could dispense with fighter protection, decided to group all the *Eindeckers* at Verdun into two independent units called Single-Seat Combat Detachments (*Kampfeinsitzer-Kommandos, or K.E.K.*). One of these, *K.E.K.* North, was located at Bantheville, a few miles northwest of Verdun, and the other, *K.E.K.* South, was located at Avillers, a few miles northeast. Boelcke asked for and received permission to establish his own *K.E.K.* in the middle, at Sivry, and scored two victories within a few days of setting up business there. The *K.E.K.* did well at first and the morale of German ground troops rose at the sight of their own aeroplanes flying over them; they were not numerically strong enough, however, to stop the French aeroplanes from coming over the lines when Colonel Barès' massive new squadrons went into action. The Germans then adopted a "barrage" policy, sending up their machines to patrol the lines endlessly in the hope that this would prevent the French from crossing over. The theory was perhaps an analogy with the army and navy principle that a line can be drawn on a map and all access to territory on one side of the line denied to the enemy, but as has been remarked the air is a big place, and it would have taken a thousand aeroplanes to form an effective barrage even on so short a front as the one at Verdun. Furthermore, the French could always score a temporary breakthrough where they wanted by massing their forces.

*   *   *

JEAN NAVARRE arrived at Verdun at the start of the battle and was assigned to one of the Nieuport *escadrilles,* N 67. On 26 February he took off before dawn on a voluntary hunting patrol of his own. Single-seater pilots had now come to be called *pilotes de chasse* or *chasseurs,* literally hunting pilots or hunters. The word *chasse* has connotations of both "hunt" and "chase" which makes it very appropriate. He spotted three German two-seaters without escort and dived on them. All three broke for home. As he closed with the

Musée de l'Air / Paris

Jean Navarre.

nearest one, the gunner in the rear seat suddenly stood up and raised his hands over his head—Navarre "captured" the aeroplane without firing a shot. He escorted his captive to Fort Rozières and flew home to breakfast. Later the same morning he took off to intercept nine enemy machines that were spotted near the field. He followed them for a time before making his move, then singled out one of them and closed in. The pilot of the two-seater accepted combat and banked hard to swing his tail out of the way and give the gunner a clear shot. Navarre rolled away, came in again and fired a short burst from close range. The two-seater turned on its back, went into a steep dive, then broke into a wild, tumbling fall and crashed into a wood. This was the first double victory of the war and it was the first time that any *chasseur* was cited in an army communiqué.

On 4 April 1916, Navarre flew three patrols in the course of which he shot down four enemy aeroplanes, an incredible performance for the time. Only one machine was officially credited as the other three fell behind the German lines.

On the afternoon of 17 June 1916, Navarre led two comrades on a patrol which started out well when they ganged up on a German two-seater engaged in artillery-spotting and shot it down. They continued the patrol and came upon another two-seater about 12,000 feet over Grand Pré, about thirty miles northeast of Verdun. The two-seater was about 3000 feet below them and Navarre waggled his wings to make sure his comrades had seen the target, then led them into a diving attack. As they closed, Navarre swung wide to distract the enemy gunner and give his comrades first shots, but the trick backfired. The German was either lucky or a first-class shot and he caught Navarre with a burst at long range. One bullet hit him, breaking his left arm and entering his side. Navarre blacked out and his Nieuport fell out of control down to about 6000 feet. He came to and struggled groggily to clear his head. He was weak and his vision was blurred. He switched off the ignition and brought the ship out of its spin, keeping its nose down and trying to spot a place to land. He landed smoothly in a playing field near a girls' school and passed out.

In the hospital he was delirious for days. He had lost a dangerous amount of blood and it is likely that some brain damage resulted. When he left the hospital he was incredibly emaciated and his constitution was so weakened that one glass of wine made him blind drunk. When his beloved twin Pierre was killed, the news was broken bluntly to Navarre and he collapsed completely. He was out of the war. Although he returned to active status in September 1918, he never flew operationally again.

*   *   *

MAX IMMELMANN was the darling of the German press. He was scoring aerial victories in the early days when each one of them was worth a headline, when each one somehow seemed no less a triumph than winning a battle or a naval engagement. Immelmann received so many fan letters (about fifty a day when he won the *Pour le Mérite*) that his batman, or orderly, became his secretary. As his flying was done in the sector of which the chief town was Lille, he was called the Eagle of Lille—*der Adler von Lille*. The R.F.C. pilots were saying that Immelmann was in every *Eindecker* from Ypres to Valenciennes and that he could somehow stay in the air for a week at a time.

The British had come up with an emergency aeroplane that they hoped would put a stop to the Fokker Scourge. The F.E.2b, known as the "Fee" and possibly the most affectionately hated and lovingly cursed machine of the war, arrived in France early in 1916 with Nos. 20, 22, 23, and 25 Squadrons R.F.C. The original F.E. was a pre-war design, but the 2b model was considerably revamped with a 160-horsepower Beardmore engine and a flexible Lewis gun in the front seat for the observer.

On 18 June 1916, three F.E.2b's were spotted crossing the lines by German ground observers. The word was telephoned to Immelmann's aerodrome and the Eagle of Lille and another pilot rushed off to try for an interception. They found the two-seaters and began fighting near Lens, a few miles southwest of Lille. Immelmann was seen to go at one Fee from the beam, fire, then zoom up into a half-loop, using his standard attack, the Immelmann turn. When his *Eindecker* slowed down at the top of the half-loop, the Fee's gunner fired one long burst. Immelmann's machine rolled over and observers on the ground saw it break up in the air and come down in pieces.

The British gave credit to the gunner in the Fee, Corporal Waller, piloted by Second Lieutenant McCubbin, No. 25 Squadron R.F.C.

Imperial War Museum / London

F.E.2b

    The Germans were shocked at the loss and talked darkly of sabotage or handed about rumors that something had gone wrong with the Fokker or that the interrupter gear was to blame. There was some mistrust of the foreigner Fokker, and of his welding technique and of his interrupter gear. Actually, Fokker had no intention of sabotaging any of his machines; the Germans were paying him well and he knew he could very easily be shot if he tried sabotage; furthermore, the welding technique was stronger than wood construction; and there was never an instance of the interrupter gear going haywire and causing a pilot to shoot off his own propeller. An official enquiry into the matter published the verdict that Immelmann's *Eindecker* had collapsed as a result of damage from antiaircraft fire.

    One very knowledgeable engineer, who was himself an ace cited for the *Pour le Mérite,* Hermann Becker, had his own theory based on personal experience and the accounts of people he knew who were there. According to Becker, Immelmann *did* shoot off his propeller, but not through any fault of the interrupter gear. The *Eindecker* Immelman was flying had just had a propeller change, and in the rush to intercept the three F.E.2b's, the machine was taken up before the mechanics could properly check the alignment of the propeller and the gun linkage. The propeller was bolted on in the wrong position and had to pass before the gun at the wrong time. Accident or defeat, the result was the same—the Eagle of Lille was gone forever.

LANOE GEORGE HAWKER was one of the most dynamic figures of the Royal Flying Corps and was the first fighter pilot to win the Victoria Cross, Britain's highest award for valor. He was born 31 December 1890, the son of Lieutenant H. C. Hawker of the Royal Navy. As a boy, Hawker was interested in all things mechanical and electrical, he had an active and inquiring mind and was fascinated by aeroplanes.

Hawker entered the Royal Military Academy at Woolwich in 1910 and in the same year joined the Royal Aero Club. He took private flying lessons with the hope of acquiring a pilot's license so that he might be accepted for the R.F.C., but had to wait until war was declared to receive a posting to a squadron. Lieutenant Hawker was assigned to No. 6 Squadron as a pilot on 5 October 1914. On 7 October the squadron flew across the Channel to Bruges. The first days of active service were hectic, for the squadron had no transport, no ground crews, no supplies, nothing. Not even a field—it operated from the race track at Bruges.

Hawker always took his revolver on reconnaissance flights and pegged a shot or two at any German aeroplanes he came across. The results were uniformly nil, but did not deter him from trying. He flew constantly, even after having received a painful wound in the leg from ground fire. For a time he had to be lifted into the cockpit.

In June 1915 Hawker was issued a fast single-seater scout, a Bristol Baby. The Baby was a pre-war racing aeroplane which might have done well in the 1914 racing season had not the war intervened. Fast, with a top speed of one hundred miles per hour, it was also maneuverable, and since the British did not as yet have a deflector gear, Hawker decided to arm it in his own way and fight with it. He had a Lewis gun fixed to the side of the

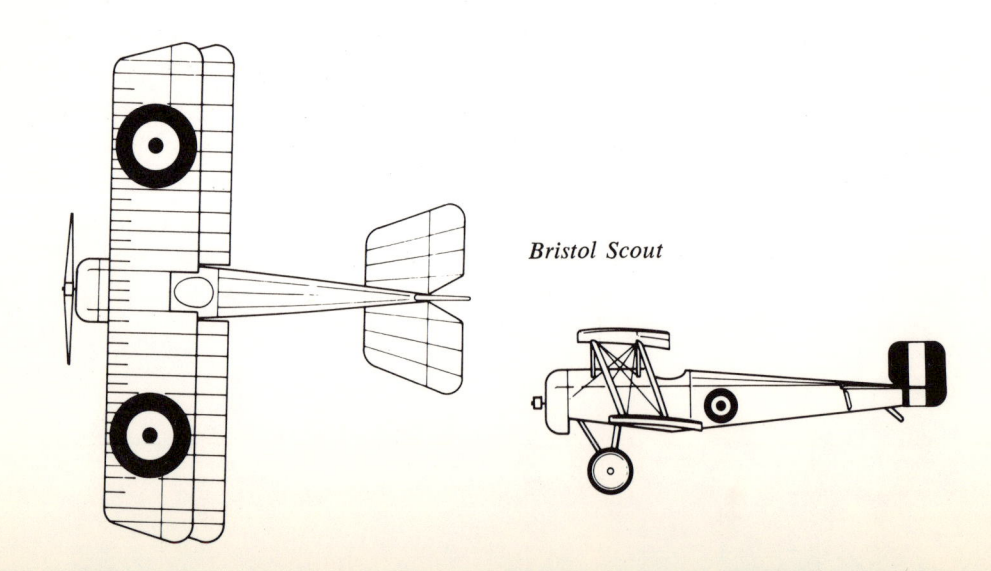

Bristol Scout

fuselage pointing down a few degrees and out to the side to clear the propeller. The idea was to come up behind an enemy aeroplane and fire a good raking burst as he swerved away.

On 25 July 1915, Hawker was flying alone on an evening patrol when he spotted a German two-seater just on the other side of the line at Passchendaele. Hawker dived at it and fired off a drum from his Lewis, but lost his target when its pilot turned and dived away. Hawker resumed his patrol and repeated the show twenty minutes later when he spotted another two-seater over Houthulst Forest. This time a British antiaircraft battery reportedly stated that he forced the aeroplane down, but the victory was not officially credited. About a half an hour later he spotted a third machine at 10,000 feet over Hooge. He closed on the machine with the sun at his back and worked his way up to within one hundred yards before he opened fire. The two-seater burst into flames, turned upside down, and crashed east of Zillebeke. The fall of the burning aeroplane was witnessed by thousands of British troops.

By August 1915 when his Victoria Cross was gazetted, or officially announced, Hawker had become an ace. When he returned home, he had completed just under a year at the Front and was one of the most experienced men in the R.F.C. He had flown every kind of mission, in every kind of aeroplane, in every kind of weather and in addition to this was an inventor. He devised new ground-air co-operation schemes, gun sights and brackets; he designed hangars and all manner of ground installations; he helped invent the metal-link machine gun belt and the double drum for the Lewis gun. His improvements and refinements permeated the R.F.C. and the inspiration of his example was ubiquitous.

In January 1916 Hawker was at Hounslow aerodrome near London to receive first deliveries of a new aeroplane, the D.H.2, which was designed and built as a fighter specifically to answer the Fokker Scourge. In his enthusiasm Hawker called the machine "a beauty," but it had some shortcomings. In the first place, the large open cockpit was so drafty that he had to design fleece-lined hip boots to protect the pilots. Secondly, and this was more serious, the 100-horsepower Gnôme rotary engines were mostly obtained from French surplus and these were not first-class power plants. They often went dead and sometimes literally came apart. Cylinders broke off the whirling engines, and when these sundered the tail booms, the whole aeroplane broke up. Hawker, however, could inspire confidence in his pilots even when they had to fly the "Spinning Incinerator."

Hawker was promoted to Major and given command of a D.H.2 squadron, No. 24, the first British fighter squadron. In February 1916, No. 24 set up shop at Bertangles near Amiens and began flying regular offensive patrols and escort missions for photographic two-seaters. Offensive patrols were those whose object was to destroy German aeroplanes on the German side of the lines. British and French tactics were developing along parallel lines as a result of infrequent though valuable inter-Allied conferences. It was at just this time that *Commandant* de Rose was putting the Nieuport *escadrilles* in the air at Verdun.

Andrews.   *Hawker.*

J. O. Andrews   *T. M. Hawker*

T. M. Hawker

Member of No. 24 Squadron and plane he crash landed.

For a time as No. 24 flew its regular escort missions things were fairly peaceful because the *Eindeckers* avoided attacking large close-flying formations. Late in April, however, the test finally came when the Germans decided that the photo-reconnaissance machines must be stopped in spite of their escort. On the day of the showdown Lieutenant J. O. Andrews was leading three other D.H.2's as escort for five B.E.2d's from No. 15 Squadron. Andrews, later an Air Vice Marshal, transferred to the R.F.C. from the Royal Scots and was an experienced combat pilot, having served at the Front in No. 5 Squadron prior to his posting to No. 24. As he led his teammates and their charges across the lines near Bapaume, a flock of *Eindeckers* appeared to the east and circled around to place themselves between the British machines and the lines, then climbed for height. When they had enough altitude, they came down on the British machines. Andrews had kept his men close to the B.E.'s, and when the *Eindeckers* attacked he turned and led his men into them head-on. The Fokkers scattered. For several moments a flurry of individual chases took place about the sky. When the Fokkers withdrew, the D.H.2's returned to the two-seaters which were carrying on with the mission. There had been no victories for either side so the fight could be called inconclusive, except that the B.E.'s finished the mission and from that moment the grip of the *Eindecker* was broken.

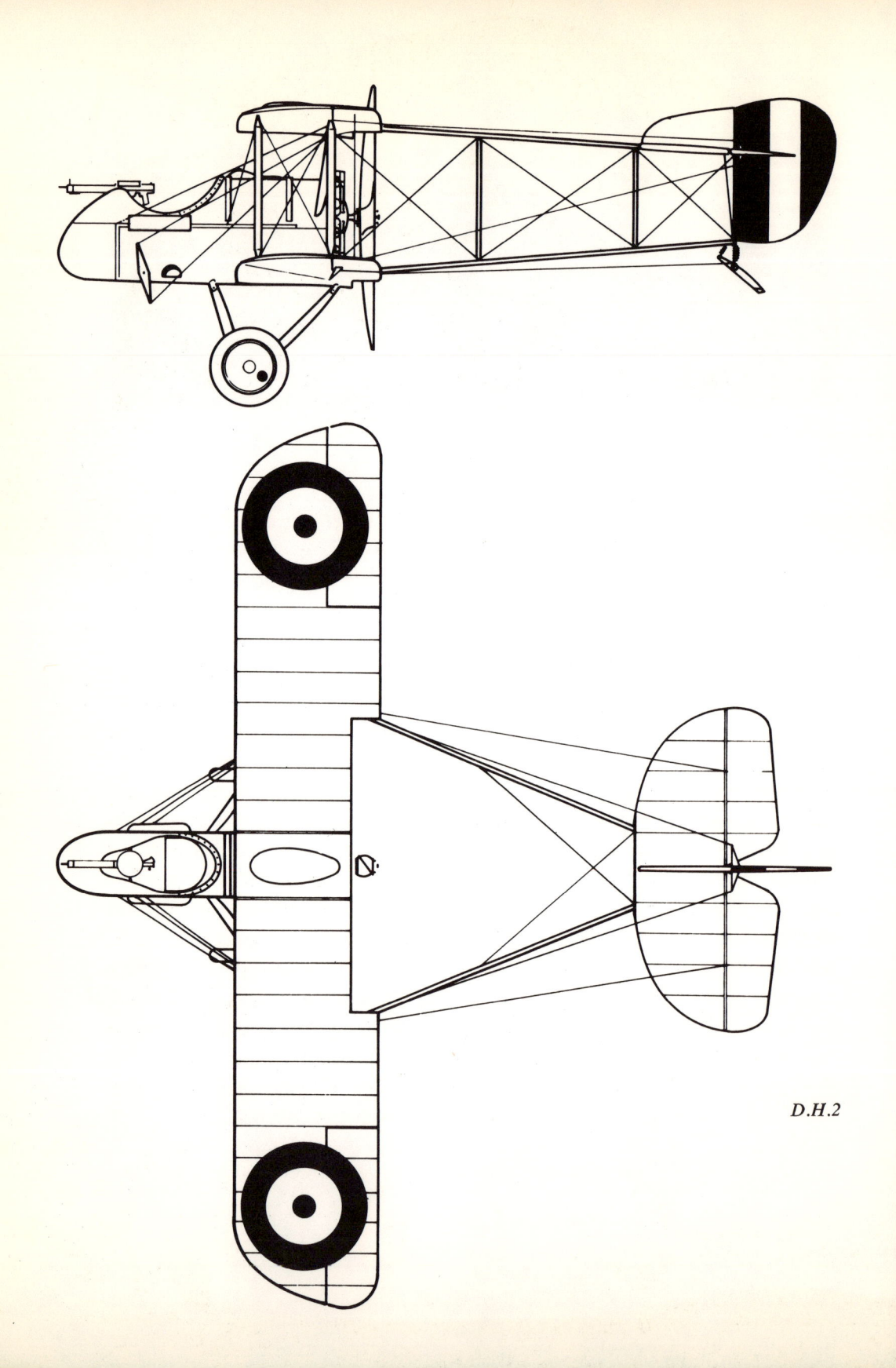

D.H.2

D.H.2

Imperial War Museum / London

An upside-down D.H. 2 that flipped during a landing.

T. M. Hawker

GEORGES GUYNEMER was born in Paris on Christmas Eve 1894. As a boy he was of a frail appearance and was much coddled by his family. There has even been a considerable amount of talk that more than his appearance was frail, that he was actually dying of consumption, or tuberculosis, when he served as a pilot during the war. The truth according to those who knew him was that he had the constitution of an ox, an assertion that the record would seem to bear out, for he was wounded on two separate occasions and was shot down no fewer than six times before he was lost in action.

Guynemer attempted to enlist immediately on the outbreak of war, but was rejected three times purely on the basis of his weak looks. It was November 1914 before he was accepted as a volunteer aviation-mechanic apprentice, a job the military acceptance boards quite rightly believed could be performed by the poorest physical specimens. With his foot thus in the door, Guynemer succeeded by sheer diligence and perseverence in getting himself enrolled for flying training. He got his brevet in April 1915, meaning he was commissioned a pilot but not an officer, and was promoted to *Caporal*, or Corporal, in May. In June he was posted to M-S 3 under *Capitaine* Brocard. The *escadrille* was at that time flying both one- and two-seater Moranes, and Guynemer was assigned to fly one of the *Parasol* two-seaters with an observer-gunner named Guerder. They scored their first victory in July, for which they were cited in the army communiqué for that day,

Guynemer and his mechanic, Guerder, at the time of their first victory.

Musée de l'Air / Paris

Musée de l'Air / Paris

Brocard.

and Guynemer was awarded the *Médaille militaire.* By the end of the year he had won another victory unaided, three more citations, and was made a *Chevalier,* or Knight, of the *Légion d'Honneur.*

Guynemer scored several more victories before he was transferred to Verdun in March 1916, but was wounded himself shortly after his arrival. In an attack on two enemy machines he made a head-on pass at one and dived under as the aeroplanes came together. The enemy gunner caught him with two bullets through his left arm and he was badly shaken up when he crash-landed behind the French lines. He spent the greater part of his recuperative leave at his father's house at Compiègne from where he would drive to the aeroplane depot at Vauciennes and inspect his *Bébé.*

In the autumn of 1916 the first of the great Spad single-seaters were issued to French *escadrilles de chasse.* Brocard's squadron, which had changed its name from M-S 3 to N 3 when it switched from Moranes to Nieuports, now became Spa 3. It was one of four squadrons known collectively as Combat Group XII, *Groupe de Combat XII.* The *Groupe* itself, comprising Spa 3, 26, 73, and 103, was known as the Storks, *les Cigognes,* and each *escadrille* bore its own variation of the Stork insignia. The Storks were named early in the war while Brocard's squadron was still flying Moranes. Who designed the first Stork insignia is not known, but he may well have been a native of Alsace or one of the northern counties where storks are common. From the middle of 1916 to the end of the war, the Storks flew Spad aeroplanes powered by the famous Hispano Suiza motors. The association grew so strong that the Hispano Suiza company adopted the stork as its trademark and uses it to this day.

There were two main variants of the Spad fighters, the S.7 and the S.13, designed by Louis Bécherau. The S.13 appeared about the summer of 1917. The Spad aeroplanes took their name from the initials of the company, *Société pour Aviation et ses Dérives,* or Society for Aviation and its Derivatives. The Hispano Suiza motors, or "Hisso" as they were called, took their name from the company founded in Barcelona by the Swiss engineer, Marc Birkigt. Hispano Suiza means "Spanish Swiss." Hisso engines were produced in great numbers at the home factory in Barcelona, and under license in France, Italy, Britain and the United States. The Spad 7 had a 140-horse-

Imperial War Museum / London

Spad 7

Musée de l'Air / Paris

Spad 7

Spad 12 with cannon that fires through opening in propeller boss.

Musée de l'Air / Paris

power Hisso to begin with and as improvements upped the rating had anywhere from one hundred eighty to two hundred horsepower. The Spad 13 had anything from two hundred to two hundred thirty-five. The Spad 7 was armed with one Vickers, the Spad 13 with two. Because of their excellent motors, their speed, ruggedness and dependability, the Spads were the finest single-seaters of the war.

A striking demonstration of the sturdiness of the Spad occurred on the morning of 23 September 1916 when Guynemer was shot down for the sixth time—demonstrating thereby his own sturdiness. Between 11:20 A.M. and 11:25 he shot down three German machines. At 9000 feet he unwittingly passed through the trajectories of French batteries and the shell from a .75 went through the water reservoir of the upper wing. Pieces of wreckage flew in all directions and the fabric of the wing ripped off. The Spad dropped in a tailspin with Guynemer struggling to regain control of his crippled ship all the way down. He managed to level off, but hit the ground hard, tore off the landing gear and the wings and caromed into the air again. He and his machine landed upside down one hundred twenty feet away. He crashed before his last victim.

"The Spad is solid," he wrote his father. "With another I would now be thinner than this sheet of paper. I landed within three hundred feet of the battery that demolished me. They weren't shooting at me, but they brought me down all the same. . . ."

*   *   *

Imperial War Museum / London

Guynemer.

Peter M. Grosz

5 / RED BARON

5

DURING THE SUMMER of 1916 it became clear to the Germans that the *Eindecker* was no longer able to match the Allied single-seaters and it was gradually withdrawn. For a time several companies produced some stop-gap machines such as the Halberstadt D II, but these were little better than the *Eindecker*. Late in 1915, however, two designers on the staff of the Albatros Works, named Thelen and Schubert, had begun work on a new single-seat scout. As with the Spad, this aeroplane's success was due to a lucky combination of airframe and aero-engine. The pre-formed plywood slabs which covered the fuselage represented a novel, not to say revolutionary, method of covering and gave to the airframe unusual strength. Various engines were fitted to the early Albatros single-seaters, but the most common was the Mercedes 160-horsepower D III, a six-cylinder in-line engine. The Germans did not develop a V-8 engine like the Hisso—all their own engines were in-line of six cylinders and many of their designs had as a consequence a long-nosed look. The new Albatros was called the D I, D indicating *Doppeldecker,* or two-winger. With 160 horsepower under the cowling, the D I was the most powerful single-seater in the German air service. It went into production at a time when an improved gun gear was available. With the extra power and an improved synchronizing gear, the Albatros D I was born just in time to become the first twin-gun fighter.

It was not so fast as the Spad 7, nor so maneuverable as the D.H.2 and the Nieuport, but the two guns went a long way to even things up. The Albatros fighters all had one weakness—their wings could be wrenched off by diving or violent maneuvering—but in the hands of competent pilots they were dangerous machines to tangle with.

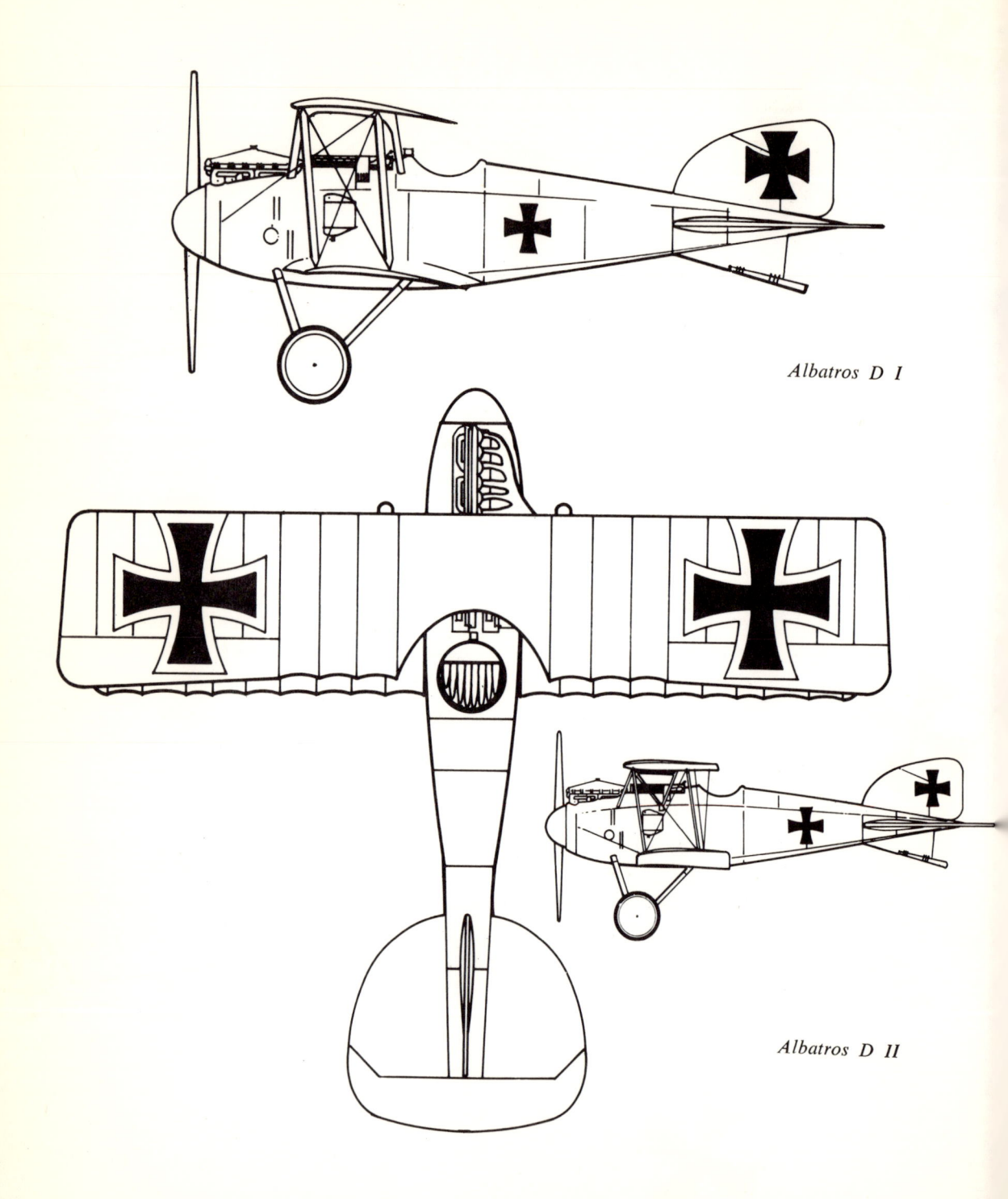

Albatros D I

Albatros D II

Halberstadt D II

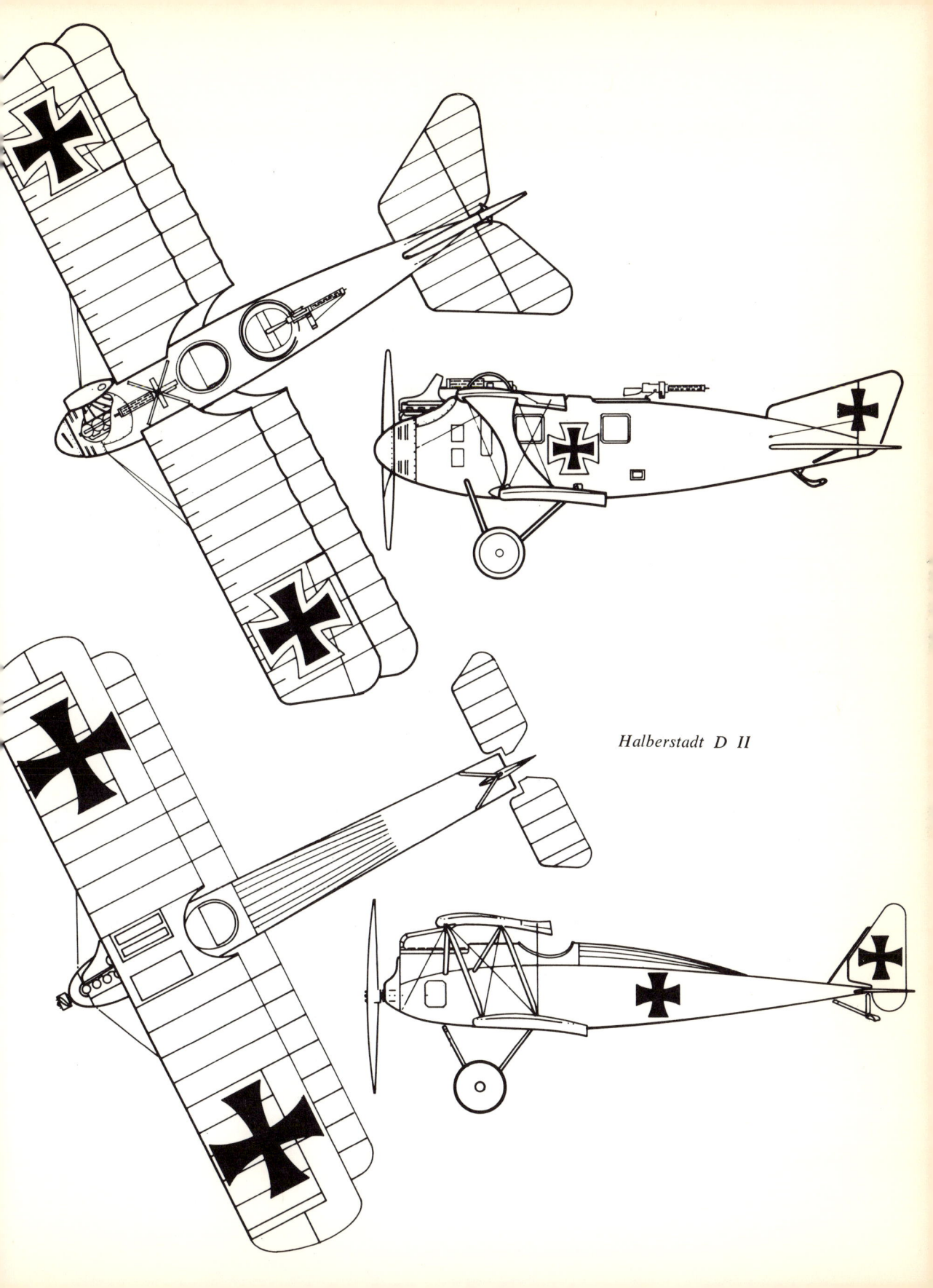

Wm. E. Morse, Jr.

Albatros D I

There was another aspect of the developing air war that made the arrival of the Albatros seem like the answer to a prayer. The early success of the *Kampfeinsitzer-Kommandos* was ascribed to the fact that the *Eindeckers* were allowed to go out hunting on their own without being tied down to the two-seaters, so it was decided to spread all-fighter units along the Front. The D I was just the machine for equipping such units, which were to be known as *Jagdstaffeln,* or "hunting echelons." Oswald Boelcke, with a score of victories, was an obvious choice to lead one of the new *Jagdstaffeln,* of which seven were originally projected. (By 1918 there were over eighty.) The standard establishment was fixed at eighteen aeroplanes, twenty-four pilots, and about one hundred thirty ground personnel. In practice the effective strength of a *Jagdstaffeln* was never eighteen machines—it was more like fifteen or twelve because of combat losses and replacement difficulties in both pilots and aeroplanes. The name was invariably shortened to *Jasta* by the pilots.

Late in the summer of 1916 Boelcke was assigned by O.H.L. to tour all fronts, report on the general state of the air service, and recommend ways and means of improving its efficiency. While on tour he kept his eyes open for promising candidates for his own *Jasta,* which was to be *Jasta 2.* At a field on the Russian Front he came across a young man he had met before, Manfred *Freiherr* von Richthofen.

Frederick the Great bestowed the title of *Freiherr,* or Baron, on the males of the von Richthofen family whose ancestors had been judges, councillors and mayors in Silesia since the seventeenth century. Manfred von Richthofen was born on 2 May 1892, the eldest son of Albrecht von Richthofen, a professional soldier. At the age of eleven he was sent to the military academy at Wahlstatt, from there to the Royal Military Academy at Lichterfeld, and from there to the War Academy at Berlin. He was graduated from the latter in the spring of 1911 at the age of nineteen. He was commissioned a *Leutnant* in the fall of 1912, while serving with the First Regiment of Uhlans, a cavalry outfit similar to the lancers. He was never a skillful horseman and he was never a really skillful pilot, but from his childhood on he seemed to have more than his share of determination. Once he put his mind to something, nothing would stop him.

On the outbreak of war, von Richthofen went with the Uhlans to the Russian Front, but was transferred within two weeks to the Western Front to serve in the Fifth Army under the Prussian Crown Prince. After a few cavalry skirmishes, the war stagnated for von Richthofen, as it did for everyone, into the trench stalemate that was to last for four more years. The cavalry was unhorsed and he became a supply officer, a job for which he had no liking. In the hope of getting some action he requested a transfer to aviation. In May 1915 he went through a four-week observer's course at Cologne and was posted to *Fl. Abt. 69* on the Russian Front. In August 1915 he was transferred to Ostend, Belgium, and shortly thereafter was transferred to Metz. On the train to Metz he spotted Boelcke and politely introduced himself. They chatted, although neither was an outgoing type, and Boelcke clearly saw that this young man was one who wanted to fight in the air but who lacked training, experience and understanding, who lacked every attribute, in fact, save one—determination.

Albatros C III

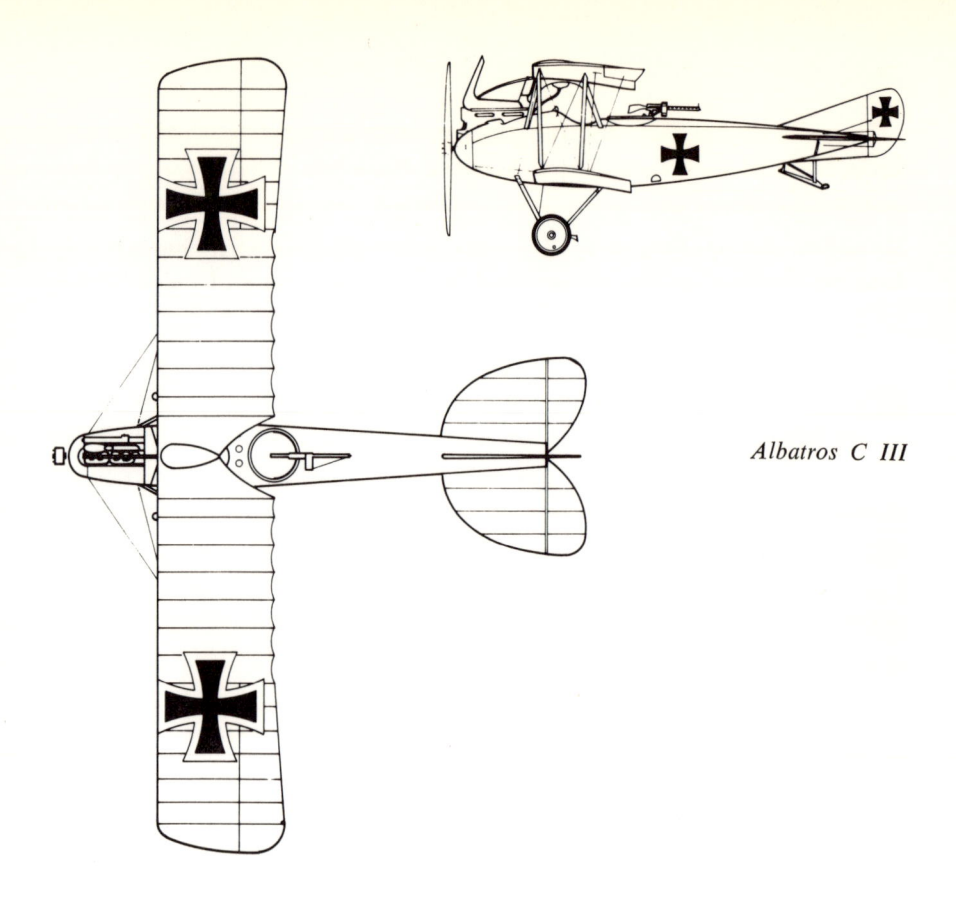

After his meeting with Boelcke, von Richthofen once more requested an instructional posting, this time for pilot training. He was accepted, sent to Döberitz, and, not without a few crack-ups, soloed on Christmas Day 1915. During the spring of 1916 he flew at Verdun as the pilot of an Albatros C III, and in the summer was transferred back to the Russian Front where he had his second meeting with Boelcke. It was at this time that Boelcke was scouting out recruits, and remembering von Richthofen asked him if he still wanted to be a fighter pilot. "Yes, sir!" said von Richthofen.

Boelcke's *Jasta 2* was stationed at Lagnicourt in northern France, a few miles northeast of Bapaume. There von Richthofen reported on 1 September. Until the middle of the month Boelcke drilled his "cubs" in the methods and techniques of air fighting, then the *Jasta* made its operational debut on Sunday, 17 September 1916.

It was a bright, clear morning as the aeroplanes were rolled out and lined up in front of their canvas tent hangars. Boelcke's cubs in their helmets and goggles, mufflers and flying suits, gathered around him for last-minute instructions and a final pep talk, then climbed into their aeroplanes. They took off, formed up into flights over the field, and headed for the lines.

Imperial War Museum / London

Albatros D II's about to take off on patrol.

Boelcke soon spotted two flights of British machines crossing the lines and heading into German territory. They were B.E.2c's with F.E.2b's for fighter escort. He guessed that the B.E.'s were on a bombing mission. Since they were heading into German territory he knew he could pick his own time to jump them. He further guessed that when they arrived over their target they would all be looking down to watch for the bomb bursts. That would be the time. He immediately began to climb to put himself and his *Jasta* above the British machines and in the glare of the sun. Over the target, which proved to be the railway yards at Marcoing, Boelcke gave the signal to attack. His *Jasta* knifed down and cut the enemy formation to ribbons. The British pilots who survived the fight reported that it was indeed a "tough lot of Huns" that had beaten them up.

Boelcke was satisfied with his team. There were losses, but by the end of October the *Jasta* was working well and he had amassed forty victories of his own. No other pilot of the time had anything like such a score. On 28 October 1916, Boelcke led the *Jasta* on five separate patrols, the last between three and four o'clock in the afternoon. Over Pozières he and his flight got in a scrap with a pair of D.H.2's from Hawker's squadron. At one point Boelcke dived on one of the D.H.2's piloted by a Canadian named Lieutenant Knight, which banked sharply to the left to elude his fire. Boelcke broke to the right and slammed his top wing against the undercarriage of one of his comrade's machines. The collision was not violent, but it apparently damaged the wing and the fabric was ripped off. Boelcke went down in wide circles—he seemed to have his machine under control. Then the damaged wing collapsed and the Albatros dropped. It hit the ground so hard it was completely demolished.

On 3 November 1916, von Richthofen shot down an F.E.2b in the morning for his seventh confirmed victory and attended Boelcke's funeral in the afternoon. Six days later he scored his eighth. Immelmann and Boelcke had both been awarded the *Pour le Mérite* for eight victories and von Richthofen confidently expected the Order himself. He was chagrined to learn that the General Staff had decided to make some reforms in the awarding of decorations. Air fighting was picking up so fast that any number of men might qualify in a short time. Germany's allies were scornfully saying that the only way to avoid winning an Iron Cross was to commit suicide. To prevent embarrassment, the required number of aerial victories a fighter had to win to earn the Blue Max was now set at sixteen.

*   *   *

THE OFFENSIVE POLICY of the R.F.C. was based on the premise that the German air service would be rendered ineffectual if the R.F.C. did all its flying on the German side of the lines. With equal or superior equipment this was a fair deduction, but in the fall of 1916 and the spring of 1917 the R.F.C. did not have equal or superior equipment. The D.H.2 was not a match for the Albatros and the pilots of No. 24 Squadron were hard pressed to hold their own. A new model of the Albatros was now in the field, the D II, with reduced gap between the wings for improved maneuverability and visibility. Hawker's squadron carried on with its offensive patrols, and as often as his administrative duties permitted, Major Hawker flew on them himself. It was forbidden for commanding officers to fly over the lines, so Hawker did his flying unofficially as an ordinary pilot and thus did not displace the regular patrol leader.

The death of Boelcke, while a blow to the *Jasta* and to the Germans generally, occurred after he had successfully launched the unit on its career, and in the month after his death the new commander, *Leutnant* Stephan Kirmaier, led *Jasta 2* to twenty-five victories in as many days. On 22 November 1916, J. O. Andrews, by this time a Captain and a flight commander, shot down Kirmaier.

Twenty-three November broke clear and cold. In the early afternoon Andrews led Major Hawker and Lieutenant R. H. M. S. Saundby (now Air Marshal Sir Robert Saundby) on an offensive patrol. Just before two o'clock

Kirmaier.

Andrews spotted two German two-seaters northeast of Bapaume at about 6000 feet. As he led his patrol down from 11,000 feet the two-seaters turned and fled. Andrews and Saundby broke off, but Hawker pressed on. When Andrews realized he had lost Hawker he turned about and headed back toward the spot where he had broken off the chase and spotted a flock of Albatros coming down on Hawker. He fired a burst at the lead aeroplane and then the Albatros were coming down on him. His D.H.2 took a burst behind the cockpit, his tanks went dry and his motor stopped. Andrews was still at about 5000 feet, and with Saundby sticking by him, he headed for the British lines. One Albatros caught up with him and fired from dead astern —his dead motor performed a valuable service and took the shots. Saundby drove off the attacker and Andrews made it to safety.

It was von Richthofen and his comrades from *Jasta 2* who had jumped the D.H.2's. Hawker had been alerted to the danger when he saw Andrews' tracers and he immediately broke off the chase of the two-seaters to face the Albatros fighters. He and von Richthofen quickly squared off and began chasing tails. None of the other Germans interferred, but stood clear and let the two settle the affair man to man. Why, no one knows for certain any more, if indeed anyone ever did. Perhaps it was because they knew von Richthofen was jealous of his victories and would resent anyone butting in; perhaps they all feared a repetition of the Boelcke tragedy when a man was needlessly lost in a wild scramble after a victim who got away anyway; perhaps this was one of the occasions when fair play and chivalry actually occurred.

Hawker and von Richthofen whirled around in a deadly merry-go-round, turning one way, then the other. They lost height, dropping to about 2000 feet, and drifting in the wind that was blowing toward German territory. Once Hawker waved. The chase settled lower and Hawker abruptly went into a loop, firing a burst at von Richthofen on the way down. Instead of pulling out he continued on down to tree-top height and started hedge-hopping for the British lines. The Albatros had the edge in speed and von Richthofen was quickly on Hawker's tail and gaining on him. He fired several bursts and finally closed to within one hundred feet where with his last burst he shot Hawker through the head. The D.H.2 tore into the water-filled shell holes just beyond the German lines, cartwheeled and broke up.

MANFRED VON RICHTHOFEN had a total of sixteen victories to his credit by January 1917 and was one of the most successful living German aces. He received his *Pour le Mérite* and was given command of his own squadron, *Jasta 11*. He was also promoted to Captain, his new rank being called *Rittmeister,* or Riding Master, since he was a cavalryman. He too received fan mail as had Immelmann and Boelcke and he had a sizeable scrapbook of newspaper clippings. He knew he had a name on the other side of the line through interviews with British prisoners. All in all, he decided it was time for him to begin asserting himself. Shortly after he took command of *Jasta 11,* he had his Albatros painted red. Aside from the personal advertising he enjoyed by using this flamboyant color scheme, it was discovered that it was much easier for the men of his *Jasta* to keep him in sight and follow his lead on operations. Bit by bit the rest of the *Jasta* adopted their leader's color and had their aeroplanes decorated with red markings of one kind or another. The practice soon passed to the rest of the German air service, or *Luftstreitkräfte,* as it was now called. The name, meaning Air Combat Force, was bestowed on the air service when it was finally recognized as an independent service and was in large measure freed from its subservience to the army.

Over thirty *Jastas* were operating on the Western Front by the spring of 1917 and the Albatros fighters dominated the scene. The D III, latest in the series, was available in considerable numbers and represented a substantial improvement over the D I and D II. The Mercedes motor was souped up by increasing the compression ratio and the horsepower was now rated at one hundred eighty. The wings had been redesigned, and while they still were not strong enough to permit reckless handling, the new "V-strut" arrangement gave improved maneuverability and rate of climb. Their morale soaring with new equipment and tough young leaders, the *Jastas* played havoc with the R.F.C., whose slow and obsolete two-seaters were still doggedly crossing over the lines in accordance with the Offensive Policy. The *Jastas* had but to wait for them and then cut them down. April 1917 was known in the R.F.C. as "Bloody April."

* * *

THE FRENCH had learned as early as Verdun the value of grouping squadrons into larger units on either a permanent or temporary basis. *Comman-*

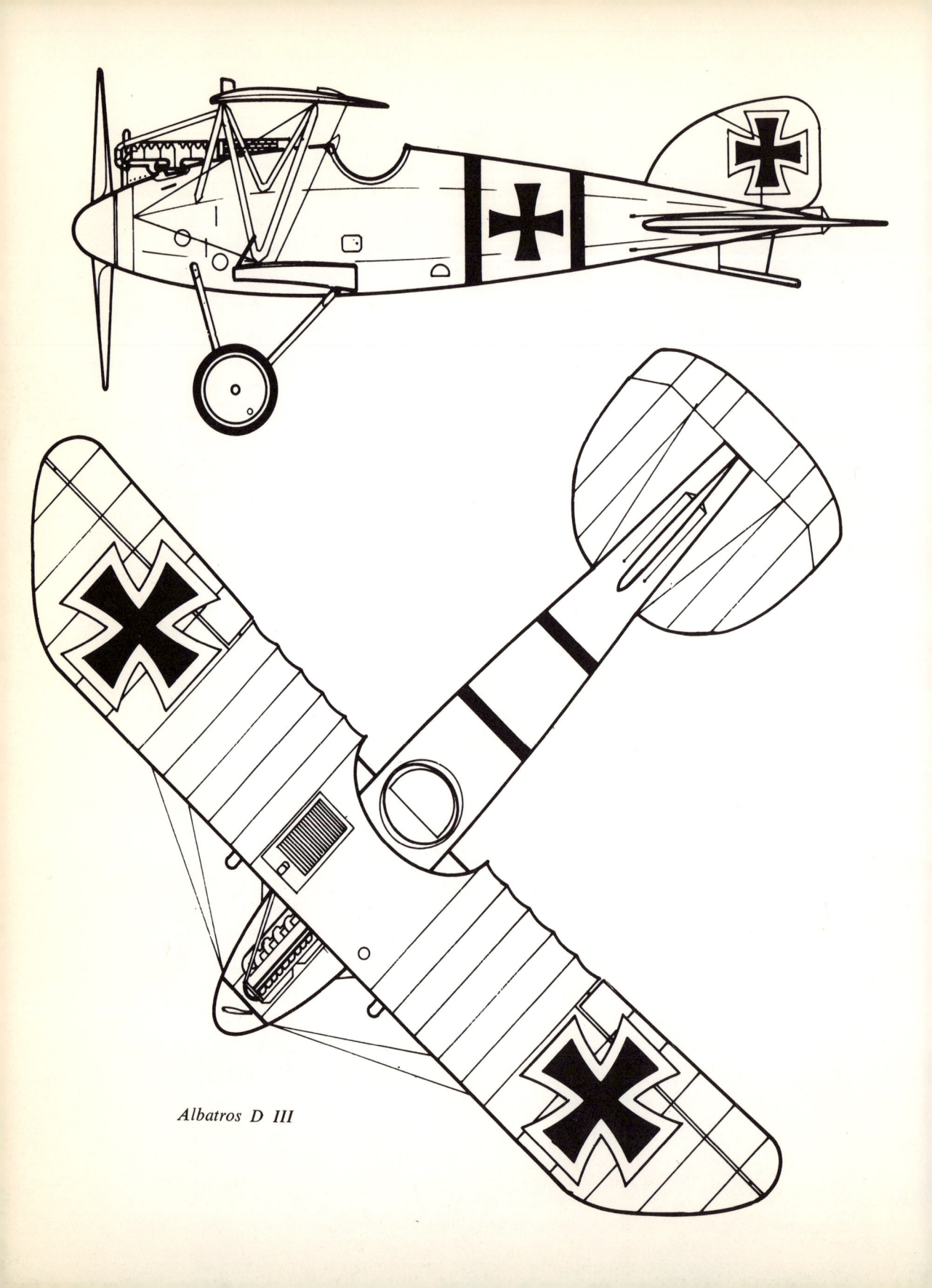

Albatros D III

Albatros D III

Wm. E. Morse, Jr.
Wm. E. Morse, Jr.

dant de Rose, who was killed at Verdun, had achieved good results by sending up machines in squadron strength and then by massing squadrons for a hard breakthrough where it was needed. The Storks, *Groupe de Combat XII*, operated as a unit for the rest of the war, shifting up and down the line as they were needed.

On 25 May 1917, George S. Guynemer, the oldest Stork and one of the youngest pilots, shot down four aeroplanes in one day while the *Groupe* was stationed near Nancy. On 11 June, with his score at forty-five, he was named an Officer of the Legion of Honor; by the end of August he was being acclaimed as the ace of aces with fifty confirmed victories.

In July the Storks transferred to St. Pol-sur-Mer near Dunkirk to take part in another muddy battle. Guynemer spent a few days at home the end of August, and returned to Spa 3 on 4 September to learn that one of his best friends, *Capitaine* Alfred Heurtaux, had been seriously wounded the day before. Heurtaux was a skilled and experienced man, a long-standing Stork ace with a score of twenty-one confirmed victories, and Guynemer was extremely upset by the news that he was wounded. Everything seemed to be going wrong. Guynemer would pace up and down fuming at bad weather, his guns would jam when he finally got in the air, and if nothing went wrong he would patrol for long hours without sighting a German aeroplane. On 10 September he had the incredible bad luck to suffer three forced landings in three different aeroplanes.

Guynemer.

Musée de l'Air / Paris

Eleven September 1917 dawned on misty and uncertain weather at the field near St. Pol-sur-Mer. The weather and the fact that he had had a bad night put Guynemer in a nervous and irritable mood. He paced about impatiently waiting for the weather to clear, and when he could stand it no longer ordered two machines made ready, one for himself and one for *Sous-Lieutenant* Benjamin Bozon-Verduraz, with whom he had been flying lately. They took off at 8:30 A.M. and headed for Bixschoote, then crossed into German-held territory near Poelcapelle. Guynemer spotted one German aeroplane far below them, a two-seater. He waved to Bozon-Verduraz and turned toward the sun, but it was hidden in cloud at the moment and there was no strong glare out of which to attack. He changed his tactics, and signalling Bozon-Verduraz to come up beneath the two-seater, indicated he would attack from the side. The crew of the two-seater were no novices, for the pilot eluded Guynemer apparently by throttling down abruptly and pulling his machine into a tight turn so that it dropped away, and the gunner got in a burst at Bozon-Verduraz on the way down. As Guynemer dived after the machine, Bozon-Verduraz spotted a flight of Albatros D III's. He feared that Guynemer might be so intent on his chase of the two-seater that the enemy fighters would take him unawares, so he turned himself to face them and opened his throttle. He went through the German formation like a shot and scattered it, the enemy pilots evidently being startled by his tactics, then he dove hard to get away. He came back up over the spot where he and Guynemer had begun the attack. The sky was empty. He hoped the Albatros were so scattered that they would not be able to reassemble their formation, and he expected that Guynemer would return soon and they could continue their patrol. Perhaps Guynemer had gotten the two-seater and his run of bad luck was finished. He circled the spot, waiting.

He waited for nearly an hour and near the end of that time, he was telling himself that each circuit would be the last, but would keep going for one more. Finally he had to return and landed at the field with his tanks nearly dry. His first words were to ask if Guynemer had gotten back yet. The answer was that he had not, and then they all knew that he was not coming back.

*   *   *

S.E. 5a

6 / "TARGET SURE"

6

THREE FAMOUS FIGHTERS appeared during 1917, the S.E.5, the Camel and the Fokker Triplane. The first two were British machines, the last German, and all three merit a brief inspection because for their day they carried specialization about as far as it could go.

The S.E.5 was the product of a unique British institution, the Royal Aircraft Factory. The Factory had its origins in the detachment from the Royal Engineers which in 1879 began experimenting with balloons at the Woolwich Arsenal. As the unit grew over the years, it gradually expanded its activities to embrace airships and aeroplanes. Before the war it was located at various sites a few miles southeast of London, at Farnborough where it finally settled permanently in 1905. None of the other major European powers had a government establishment producing aeroplanes, so the Factory frequently came under fire on the grounds that it represented Government competition with private enterprise. It is true that the Government caused too many obsolete designs to be produced, and Bloody April was the disaster it was because British air crews were being sent out in Factory aeroplanes, the B.E.'s, R.E.'s, and F.E.'s, but it is also true that the Factory's S.E.5 was and is one of the classic aeroplanes of all time. Whatever the Factory's critics said, the S.E. was one of the finest single-seaters of the war.

The S.E.5 first went into action in March 1917, the S.S.5A in June, and about 5000 of these stable, sturdy and angular aeroplanes were built by the Factory and its subcontractors. The difference in the two models was in the power plant, for the construction and general arrangement were the same. Construction was all-wood and the aeroplane was completely covered

Cockpit area and armament of S.E. 5a.

with fabric except for the aluminum radiator and plywood panels around the motor. In the S.E.5 the 150-horsepower V-8 Hispano Suiza was standard, while the S.E.5a had the 200-horsepower Wolseley Viper, a British version of the Hisso with an increased compression ratio. With the Viper the S.S.5a was the fastest single-seater at the Front, its top speed at ground level being just under one hundred forty miles per hour. The S.E. was the first British fighter to be armed with two guns, a Lewis mounted on the top wing and fixed to fire over the propeller and a synchronized Vickers mounted on the top left side of the fuselage. The S.E. and the Spad were both strong, fast aeroplanes whose pilots could dive them hard to attack or escape, confident that no German pilot dared dive so hard in an Albatros or Fokker for fear of leaving his wings behind.

S.E.5a

U. S. Air Force

S.E.5a

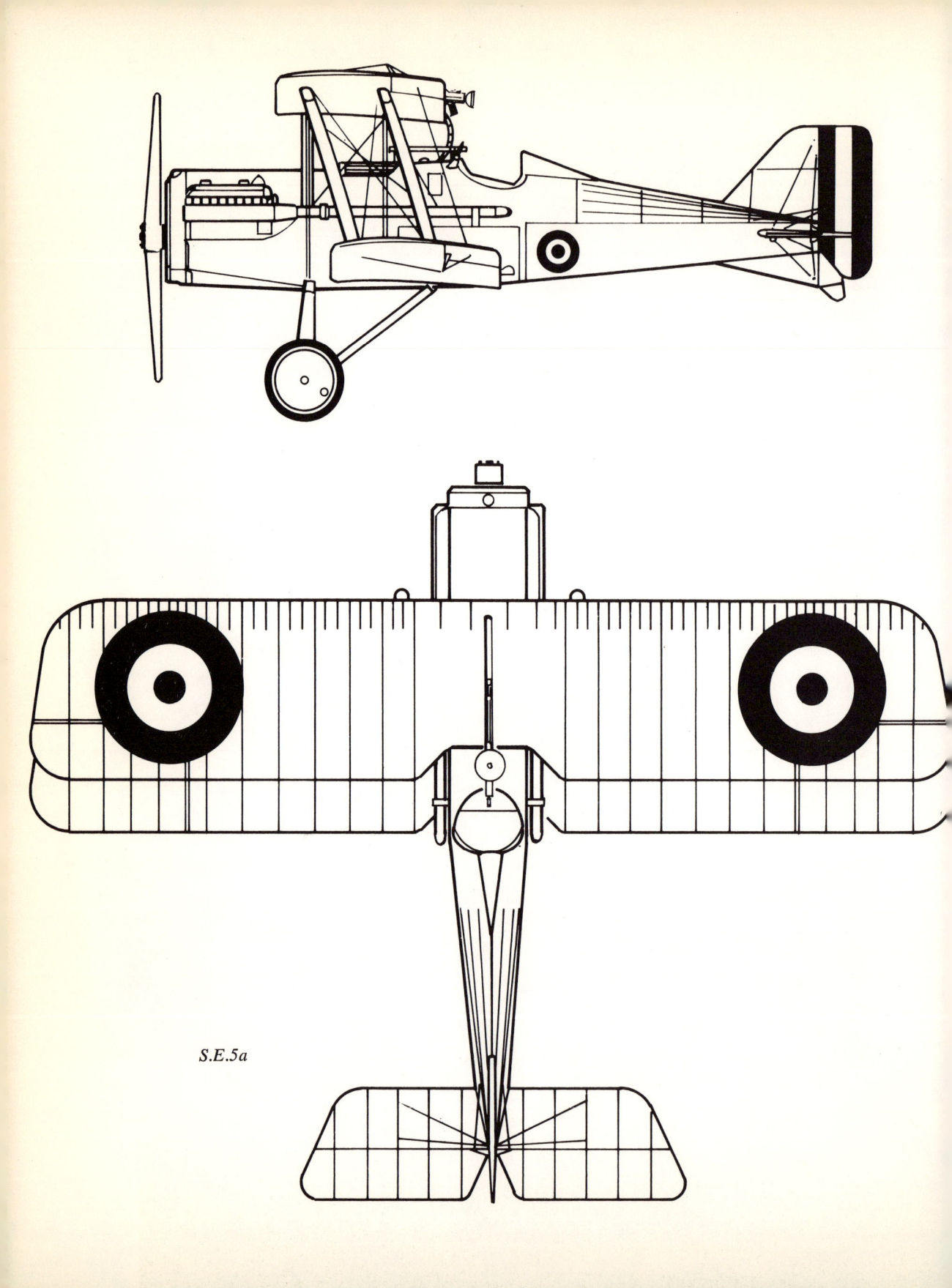

The second of these three famous aeroplanes was the Sopwith Camel, the first British single-seater to be armed with *twin* guns—a year after the Albatros. The guns, synchronized Vickers, were mounted atop the engine cowling in a faired metal housing and it was this hump that gave the Camel its name. Nearly 5500 were built, and between July 1917 and the end of the war Camel pilots scored 1300 victories.

The Camel was sometimes called a "tricky beast" because it was very sensitive on the controls and because it spun easily. The latter characteristic was chiefly the result of the combination of rotary engine and short fuselage. The torque or twisting effect of the 130-horsepower Clerget rotary caused the Camel to drop its nose in right-hand turns. Unless the tendency were corrected with a little opposite rudder, the nose would continue to drop until suddenly the tail whipped around and the aeroplane was spinning. The rotary engine had a temperamental tendency to choke if the fuel-air mixture were too rich, especially on take-off, and the pilots had to be careful with the mixture control. Stalls on take-off caused many accidents among Camel students, for when the motor choked the aeroplane stalled, and a stall was always followed by a spin. It is easy to recover from a spin if there is room under the aeroplane to let it fall a bit, but on take-off the room isn't always there. The problem was similar to the one that caused the D.H.2 to be called the Spinning Incinerator. All the Camel asked, however, was that the pilot keep on his toes. In return for this it offered him a swift, sure mount, the proof of whose excellence is the number of victories scored by Camel pilots, the highest number attributed to any combat machine of the war.

Sopwith Camel

U. S. Air Force

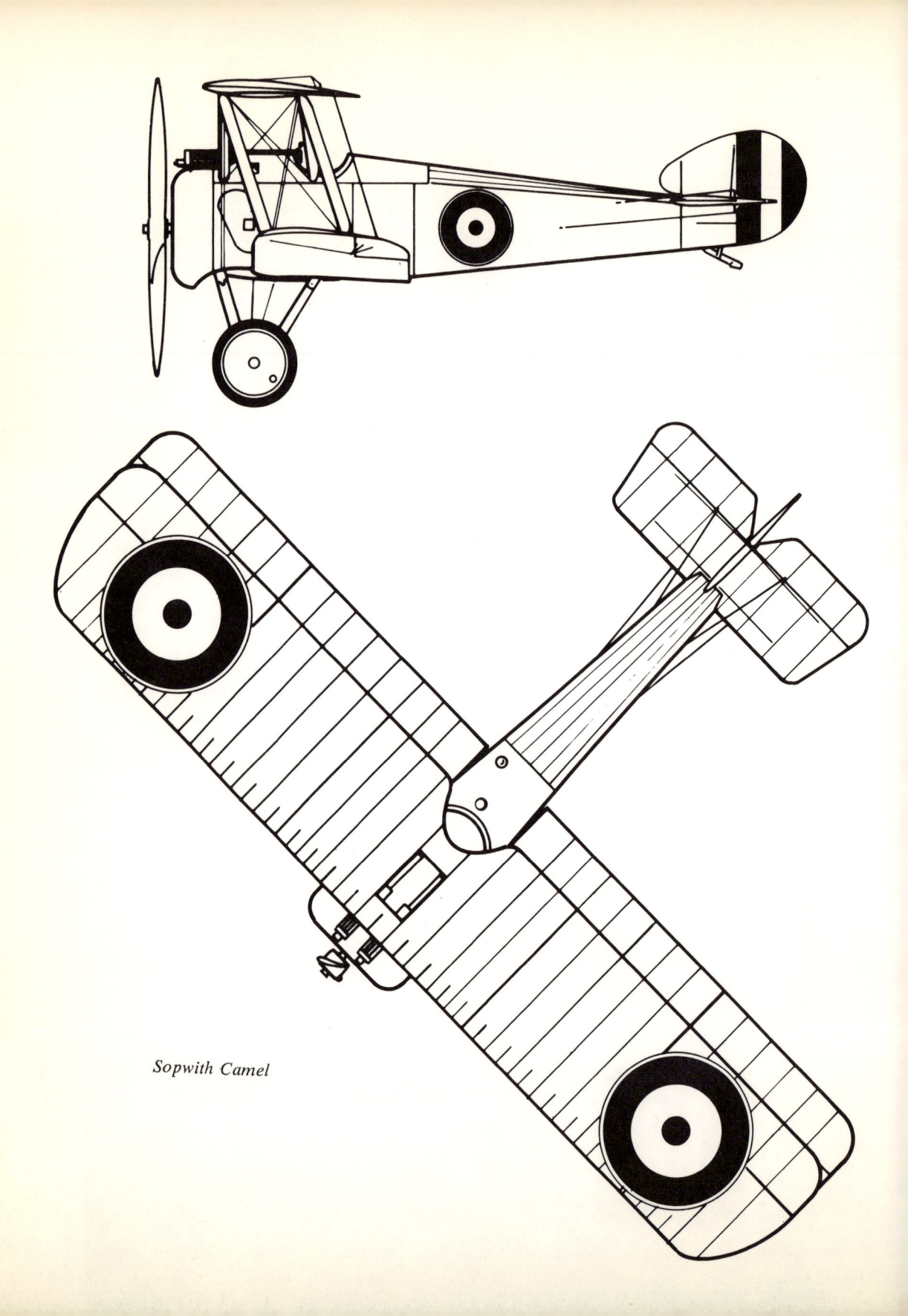

Sopwith Camel

Sopwith Camel.

U. S. Air Force

A famous ace—Major Billy Barker—and his Camel.

Imperial War Museum / London

On the other side of the fence, things were going slowly for Tony Fokker. His chief designer, Martin Kreutzer, was killed in a flying accident in the summer of 1916, and since the *Eindecker* had gone out of favor the company had produced little more than a biplane version of it. Fokker was lucky enough to have on his staff at this time a young man who was to put him back in business. Reinhold Platz had been with Fokker as a welder since 1912 and had done a little bit of just about everything in the shop. He was working as Kreutzer's assistant when he was killed and was the best man to step into his position, but although he remained with Fokker as his chief designer for nearly twenty years, he was never acknowledged as such. Fokker always liked to claim he designed his own aeroplanes. The remarkable thing

Sopwith triplanes

Imperial War Museum / London

Sopwith triplanes

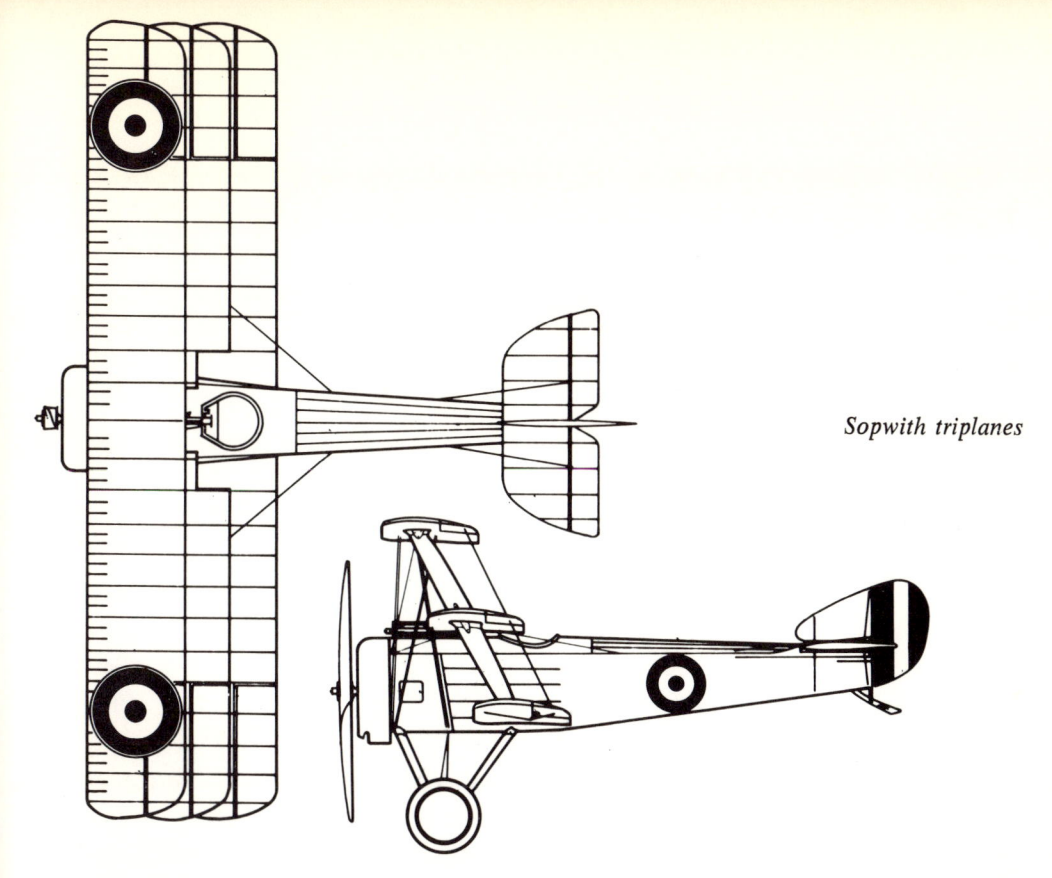

about Platz, who died in 1966, was that he had no aero-engineering training—he picked up what he knew by working with Kreutzer, or by experimenting or by instinct.

During the spring and summer of 1917 the British Royal Naval Air Service operated several fighter squadrons equipped with the Sopwith Triplane on the Western Front. This machine did so well for the Naval pilots that many constructors on both sides tried their hands at producing triplane or even quadruplane designs. The Sopwith Triplane was replaced by the Camel in the summer of 1917 and the triplane craze died away, but it could be argued that the Triplane was not so good as it seemed and that the credit for its success really belongs to the men who flew it. A Canadian named Raymond Collishaw, for example, who is now a retired Air Vice Marshal, commanded "B" Flight in Naval Ten Squadron during the period of 1917 when the unit flew the Triplane, and he and his pilots scored eighty-seven victories between the months of May and July.

Fokker decided he wanted to try a triplane design, so with no discussion he simply told Platz to start work on one, instructing him to use the 110-horsepower Oberürsel rotary engine. The Oberürsel was a German version of the French Le Rhône produced under license by the Motorenfabrik Oberürsel, a company Fokker happened to own, and it was a second-rate motor. It was so bad, in fact, that, whenever possible, captured French Le Rhônes were substituted for it. Even with its poor motor, however, the Fokker Triplane was a resounding success, largely because it was the first combat machine to which Platz was able to make a substantial contribution.

The wings of the Fokker Triplane were its most interesting feature. Although there were three wings on this unusual machine, their total area was actually less than that of contemporary biplanes. Wing area of the Triplane was two hundred square feet as against two hundred thirty and two hundred fifty in the Spad and S.E.5 respectively. This reduction of supporting surface was made feasible by the light weight of the aeroplane—it weighed 1200 pounds while the S.E.5 and Spad weighed about a ton—and the light weight was made possible by the steel-tubing construction that was a Platz trademark. (In 1918 when the Fokker D VII designed by Platz was being rushed into production, a subcontractor, Albatros, built one experimental model entirely of wood instead of steel tubing—it was heavier by forty pounds.) Platz improved on everything. He enclosed the axle of the landing gear with a large wing-like fairing, with fully a third the area of the lower wing, which had enough lift to offset the weight of the landing gear. He employed a very thick aerofoil section on all three wings which, while it increased drag, considerably increased lift efficiency. The fuselage of the Triplane measured about eighteen feet and was shorter than that of the Camel.

The Triplane was slow because of the poor motor and the thick wings, but because of the high lift of the thick wings it had an excellent rate of climb, and because the wings and fuselage were short and the motor was a rotary, it was fantastically maneuverable. The machine was officially labelled Dr I, Dr for *Dreidecker,* or three-winger, and I for the first Fokker triplane design.

The Triplane was introduced the end of August and the beginning of September 1917 and was gradually withdrawn during the spring of 1918.

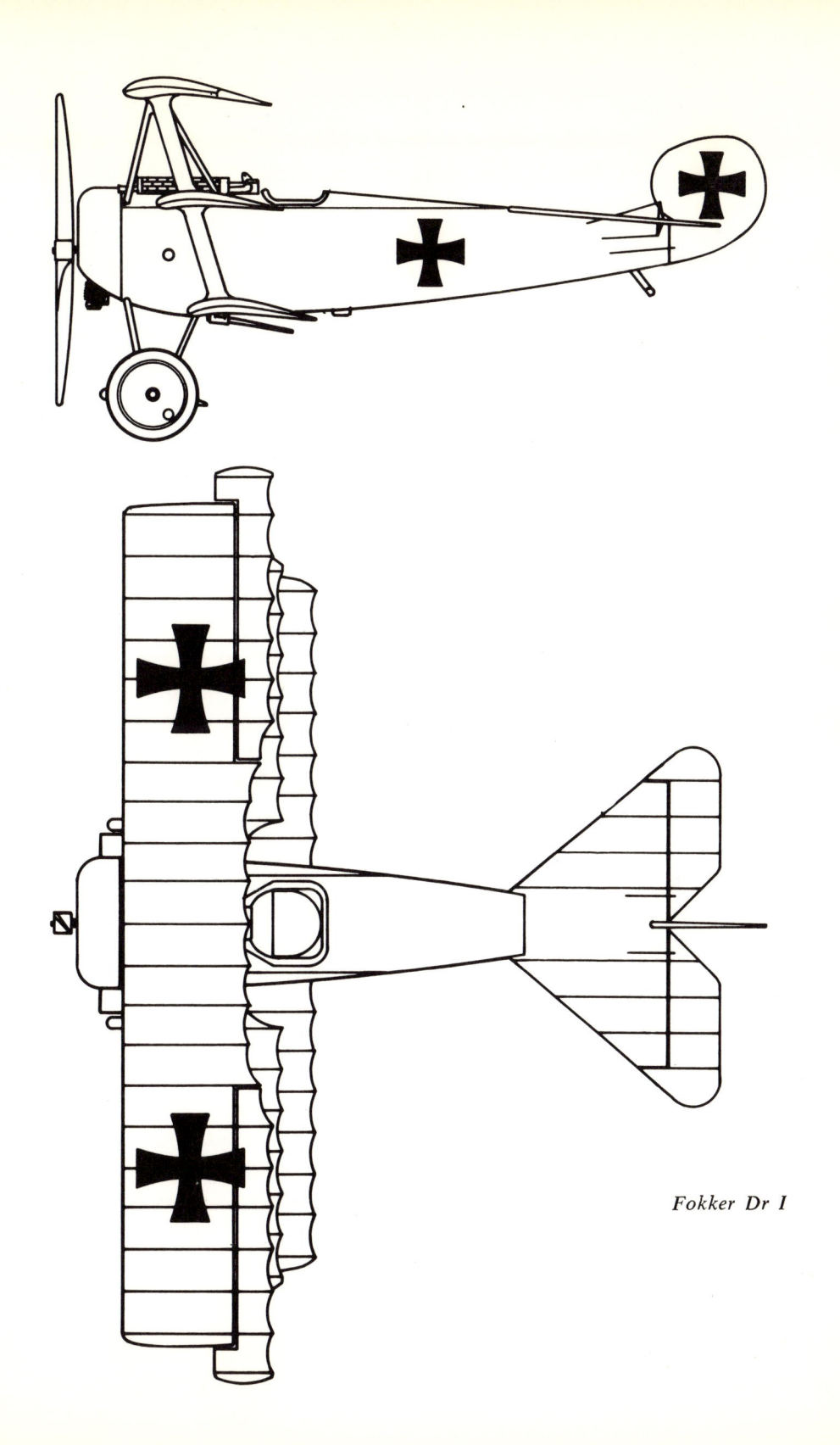

Fokker Dr I

Peter M. Grosz

Fokker Dr I

Its active career was not much longer than that of the Sopwith Triplane, but in those few short months it became one of the best-known machines of the war. Again like the Sopwith Triplane, it was flown by some of the most expert pilots of the time—von Richthofen, Udet, Loewenhardt, Voss —and not the least among them was the commander of *Jasta 12, Leutnant* Herman Becker. Becker, who lives today in West Germany, had flown many missions as a bomber pilot when he transferred to fighters. By the spring of 1918 he was an experienced, combat-wise veteran who knew how to get the best out of his machines and who lived by his own set of rules: *"Never show your back to the enemy. Always keep looking around. Always attack fast and break away fast. Always try for surprise. Always get in close to fire—fifty feet or less."* When he commanded his own squadron, Becker continually exhorted his men to follow his rules.

The maneuverability of the Fokker Triplane made it the perfect weapon for his tactics. One day he met a French Spad head-on in a challenge of nerves. He and the French pilot flew straight at each other, each held his fire. At the last second they each rolled to the right to avoid a collision.

Peter M. Grosz

Fokker Dr I

They pased so close Becker could feel the wind of the other's passing. He pulled his Triplane around in a tight turn and because it was so handy he was almost on top of the Spad before its pilot had begun to turn. He fired at point-blank range right into the cockpit. The pilot had had one chance, to dive. He hadn't taken it so he was done for. No machine could turn inside the Triplane.

"Target-sure," Becker used to say, "so close that every burst is target-sure. That this may happen to oneself must not deter one. Whoever has the stronger nerves is the victor."

*   *   *

Fokker Dr I

Wm. E. Morse, Jr.

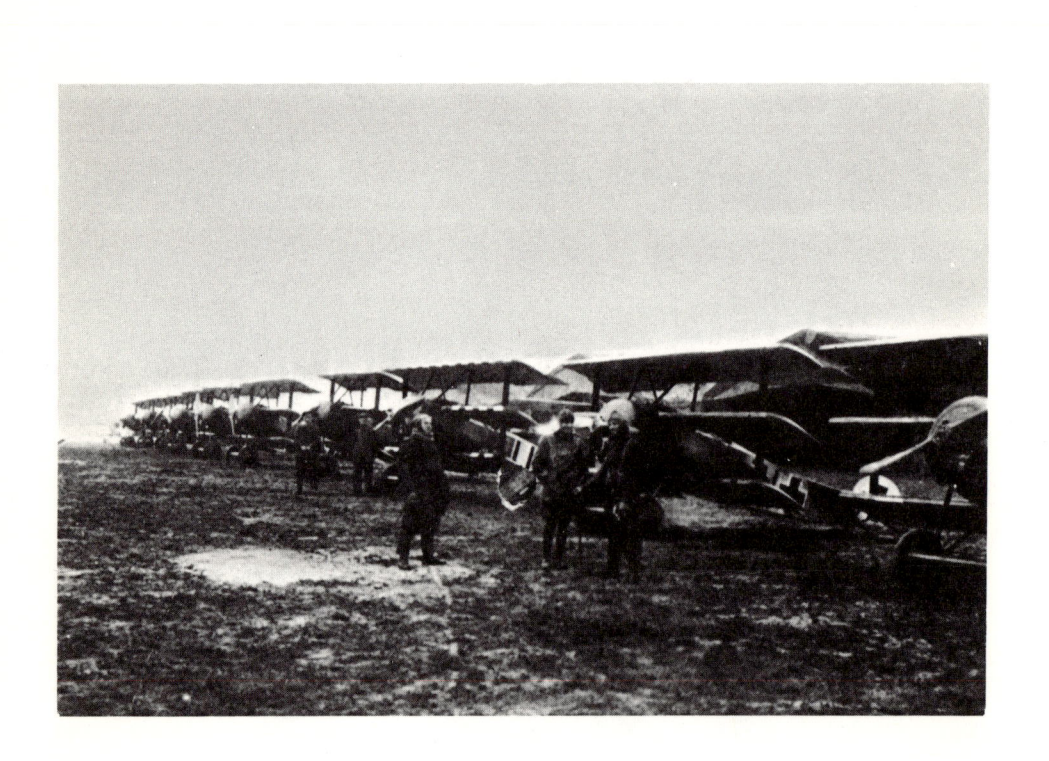

7 / VICTIMS AND VOLUNTEERS

7

THE ROYAL AIR FORCE came into being on 1 April 1918, when the Royal Flying Corps and the Royal Naval Air Service were combined into an independent service. Major General Sir John Salmond was appointed Commander in Chief of the R.A.F. on the Western Front.

Former R.N.A.S. Squadron No. 9, which now became No. 209 Squadron R.A.F., was a Camel squadron, led by Squadron Commander C. H. Butler and based at Bertangles. Deputy Commanding Officer was Captain A. Roy Brown, a Canadian.

On 21 April 1918, fifteen Camels of No. 209 took off on a high offensive patrol. Captain Brown was leading the first flight and was in overall command of the patrol; the second and third flights were led by Captains O. W. Redgate and O. C. Le Boutillier respectively. In Brown's flight of five aeroplanes were an experienced man and a new man. The former was Lieutenant F. J. W. Mellersh, who finished the war with a score of nine confirmed victories and eventually rose to the rank of Air Vice Marshal, winning a knighthood as Sir Francis. The latter was Second Lieutenant Wilfred R. May, a Canadian like Brown who was on his first offensive patrol. May was to win the D.F.C. (Distinguished Flying Cross), a Captaincy, and seven confirmed victories by the end of the war, but on the morning of 21 April all that was ahead of him. He had everything to learn; he had been told to stay out of a general scrap should one develop, to stay above and watch, to dive and run for home should he get into trouble.

The squadron got off the ground about 9:30 A.M. and patrolled for some three-quarters of an hour before getting a sighting. It was a pair of German two-seaters, and Le Boutillier's flight broke away to give chase. The other two flights, led by Brown, continued their patrol, reaching the end of their beat several miles south of the River Somme near Corbie. Two machines dropped out with engine trouble and returned to base. Brown now led a half-strength squadron of eight aeroplanes in a northerly direction toward the Somme, Le Boutillier and his flight following several minutes behind.

On 21 April 1918, at about the time that Brown was taking off with his patrol, Manfred von Richthofen was giving his pilots the once-over before leading them off on a similar free-lance rover. He was to lead the famous Triplanes of *Jasta 11* plus a flight of Albatros D V's from *Jasta 5*. Among the new members of his unit whom the *Rittmeister* would be keeping an eye on, was a cousin, *Leutnant* Wolfram von Richthofen. This was to be his first patrol. Wolfram von Richthofen had been given just about the same instructions as Wilfred May. Wolfram followed his; Wilfred didn't. The flights shaped up in the air, then von Richthofen led them west along the Somme valley.

As Brown led his patrol north toward the Somme at about 12,000 feet, von Richthofen led his west along the Somme at about 3000 feet. Near Cérisy, a hamlet on the left bank of the Somme, British antiaircraft gunners spotted the German fighters and opened up at them. Brown spotted the familiar white puffs and turned toward them, almost immediately catching sight of the German machines. He waggled his wings and dived to the attack. At the same moment the German pilots caught sight of the Camels and rose to meet them.

From 12,000 feet seven stubby olive-drab Camels howled down. May stayed behind—to watch. The flashy German "Circus" machines—white, red, yellow, green, blue—reared up and the patrols came together. Machine guns crackled as the pilots squeezed off their first shots simultaneously. When they came together at a combined speed of two hundred miles an hour they broke left or right, up or down, or went through each other's formation, then whipped around trying to get on somebody's tail. Le Boutillier and his flight caught up and waded in. A blue-tailed Triplane was seen to dive straight down out of the fight, Lieutenant Mellersh on his tail. Two more Triplanes dived after Mellersh.

Second Lieutenant May circled above and watched. He saw the head-on

Albatros D V

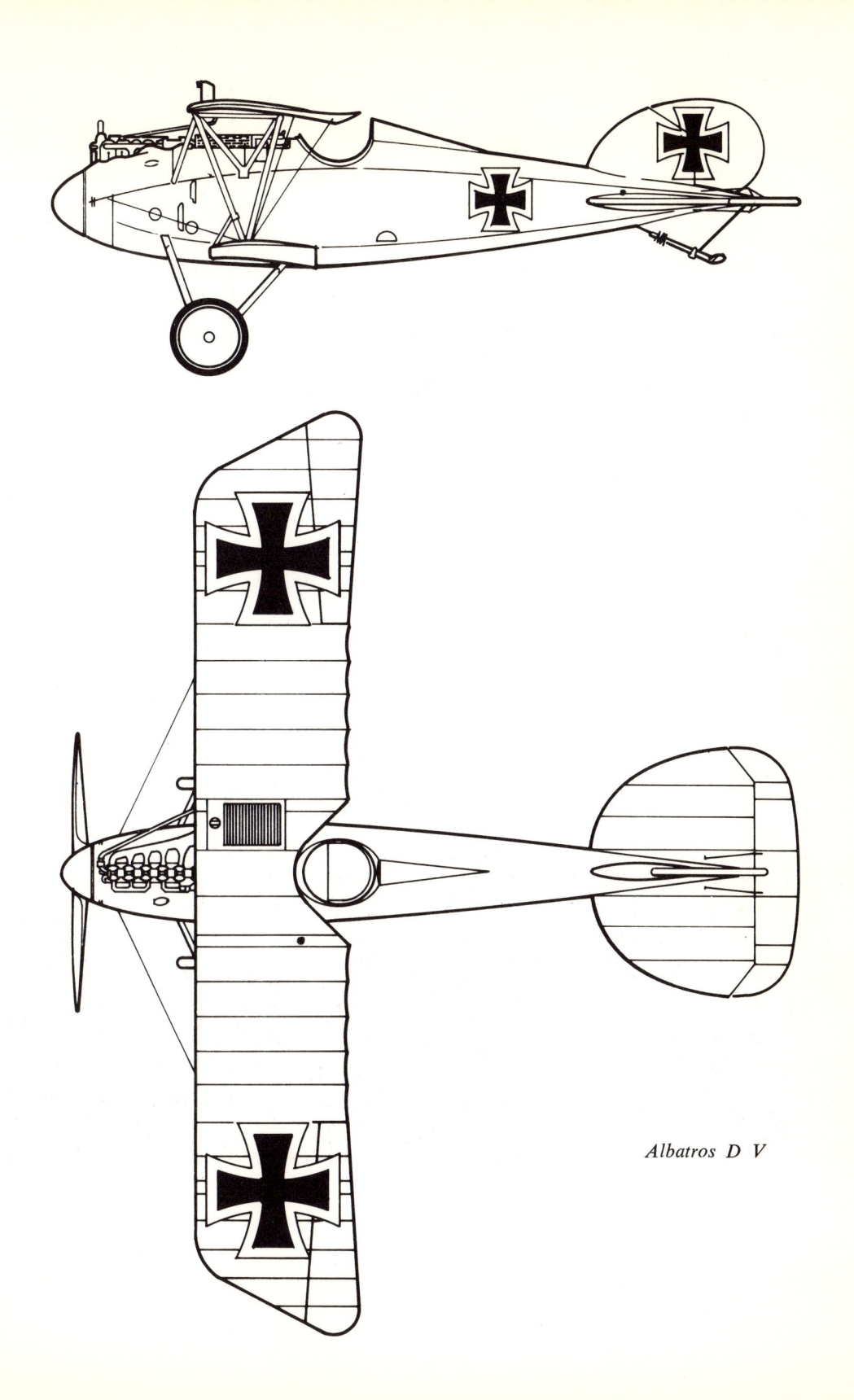

attack, saw the aeroplanes start their tail-chasing whirlwind, saw the fight settle lower and drift westward in the wind. A German machine rose up out of the fight and arched back down into it. May watched. The first Hun he had ever seen. Another one! He dived at it. It was too much to expect him to stay out of it. He followed his man down, fired and missed, plunged on down into the scrap. Suddenly Tripes seemed to be coming at him "from all sides." He later said that he had the impression that he was at the center of a ring of German machines that had only one target, and that he "seemed to be missing some of them by inches." In his excitement he held his guns open and fired one continuous burst, hoping to spray all of them, until his guns jammed. So far, he had forgotten everything he had been told. At this

The Red Baron (left) *chats with his men.*

Imperial War Museum / London

point he remembered one thing—how to get out. He wrenched his machine into a spin and dropped away toward the earth. He caught a quick glimpse of the sun as he leveled out and promptly set a course west. He looked about as he headed home, saw no enemy machine following him, and began to feel pretty good that he had gotten away.

Roy Brown saw May drop away from the fight. He only had time for a glance, then he had his hands full. He shook off two pursuers on the fringe of the "dogfight," then glanced around again for May. He spotted him low down and heading for British territory. He also saw that a red Triplane was sitting on May's tail.

May didn't know he was being pursued until he heard the rip of machine guns. Frantically he turned and dived, coming out directly over the village of Vaux-sur-Somme, where the tiles were nearly blown off the roofs by the passing of his Camel and the red Tripe. They thundered over the village and skimmed the hill behind it, the guns of the Triplane snapping off short bursts at close range. May turned as he reached the Somme and headed down the river valley. The red machine was directly behind and slightly above May, outguessing him at every turn, closing the distance with every evasion May tried. In a few seconds May would be trapped between the rows of bare trees lining the banks of the Somme. He went around a sharp bend in the river, but the red Triplane beat him to it by leaping over a hill and May was "as good as in the bag."

Lieutenant Mellersh was so closely pursued by the two Triplanes that the only way he could escape was to throw his machine into a spin and let it drop. He pulled out low down and found he had shaken off the two Huns. His course took him over the Somme not far from the sharp bend, and as he glanced around he spotted Brown's Camel over it and, north of it, a red Triplane.

When Brown spotted the red Triplane on May's tail, his reaction was instantaneous—he went for it. He put his nose down in a shallow dive and covered the distance in a minute, coming out at about two hundred feet to one side of the two aeroplanes. He banked quickly and got in one burst at the red machine. He crossed behind them and brought his Camel around to have another go. The other two aeroplanes were so low that he momentarily lost sight of them behind the trees. When he caught sight of them again they were still apparently zig-zagging, the red machine hot on May's tail. By flying a straight course while they were zig-zagging and turning about, Brown caught up with them again. It is conjectured that at this point he may have fired a second burst at the red Triplane, for it was then that Mellersh saw Brown's Camel close to it.

The red machine abruptly wobbled, swerved and went down on a more or less even keel, landing upright about a mile northwest of Vaux-sur-Somme. The undercarriage collapsed under the impact, but the machine was otherwise intact.

The pilot of the red Triplane was indeed von Richthofen, and a hasty examination revealed that one small-calibre bullet had killed him. But for fifty years the vexed question of who killed von Richthofen has been kicked about, tossed about and argued about, and the signs are that the controversy will never be resolved. For was it really von Richthofen's Triplane that Brown fired at? Brown did not mention him by name in his combat report—he merely said that he had fired at a "pure red Triplane" that was firing on May and was seen to crash by May and Mellersh. Also, as most of the chase took place close to the ground, several ground gunners took a shot at the red Triplane as it went by. Three Australian gunners in particular were honestly convinced that one or the other of them had brought it down. They were Sergeant C. B. Popkin, Gunner W. J. Evans, and Gunner Robert Buie. Whether the red Triplane referred to in Brown's combat report was indeed von Richthofen's machine or not is the critical point, and one for which no absolute proof seems to exist. Numerous officers and men of the Australian Corps, in whose lines von Richthofen crashed, insisted that his machine came under ground fire only.

It is most ironic that with all the shooting only one bullet apparently hit the Red Baron, and that small-calibre bullet could have come from anywhere.

The following afternoon, 22 April 1918, the *Rittmeister* was buried by No. 3 Squadron, Australian Flying Corps, with military honors.

* * *

IN APRIL 1916 the French air service established N 124 on the roster of *escadrilles* on active duty. The unit was named *Escadrille Américaine,* and except for its French officers and ground crew was composed of volunteer Americans. A number of Americans in France when the war began promptly joined the Foreign Legion, but Norman Prince of Massachusetts wanted to form an all-American flying squadron. The idea at first met with a cool reception, but after a year of war the French Government began to think the American Government needed some prodding to take a more decisive part in the Allied effort, and so permitted the formation of such a unit for its propaganda value. Whether or not the *Escadrille Américaine* speeded America's entry into the war, it definitely had propaganda value. Norman Prince enlisted valuable support from Dr. Edmund Gros, one of the heads of the American Field Service, and on 20 April 1916, at Luxeuil-les-Bains, the squadron "was officially received among the French arms," as the memorial plaque at Luxeuil says.

Student pilots of the Lafayette Flying Corps.

Paul A. Rockwell

Nieuport 17

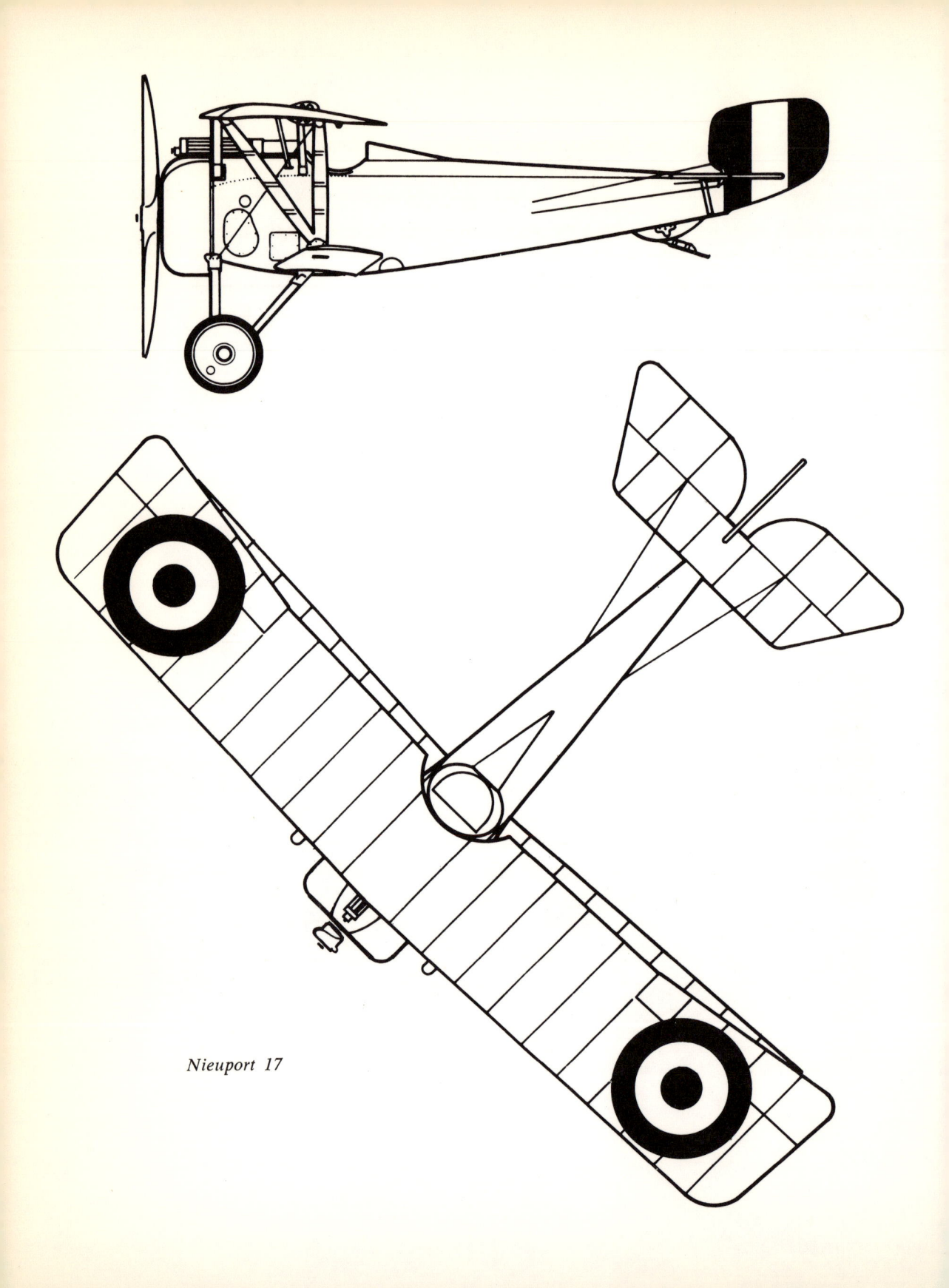

Almost immediately the German ambassador in the United States lodged a protest against neutrals taking part in the war, so the name was changed as a cover-up. *G.O.G.* suggested *Escadrille des Volontaires,* but the Americans didn't like the name because it was too vague. Someone suggested *Escadrille Lafayette* after the French general who fought in the American Revolutionary War; the Americans liked the name with its implication that they were repaying France a favor. The name was submitted to the French Government and accepted.

Not all Americans who volunteered for flying duty were sent to the Lafayette Escadrille—it was only one squadron and could not absorb that many men. A total of thirty-eight Americans served in the unit, and about one hundred sixty others served in various units as volunteers before the United States entered the war. The American volunteers were known collectively as the Lafayette Flying Corps, whatever squadron they served in. Some preferred to remain in their French squadrons when the United States Air Service finally arrived on the scene. On 18 February 1918, the *Escadrille Lafayette* was absorbed by the United States Air Service as the 103rd Pursuit Squadron.

During its existence as a French unit, in other words for as long as it was called *Escadrille Lafayette,* its pilots scored thirty-eight victories, seventeen of them being achieved by a Frenchman named Raoul Lufbery. One of the unit's French officers, *Lieutenant* Alfred de Laage de Meux, scored three victories, as did Norman Prince. Two victories each were scored by Kiffin Rockwell, William Thaw and Bert Hall. Hall wound up in a federal penitentiary for a swindling rap a few years before World War II. One victory each was scored by James Norman Hall, Willis B. Haviland, Charles C. Johnson, Henry S. Jones, Walter Lovell, Didier Masson, Kenneth Marr, Edwin C. Parsons and David Peterson.

*   *   *

Lafayette Escadrille aerodrome.

U.S. Air Force

8 / COMPLETING THE CIRCLE

8

THE UNITED STATES AIR SERVICE was slowly pulling itself together. In May 1918, a Division of Military Aeronautics directly responsible to the Secretary of War was finally established; until then the aviation service was merely a branch of the Signal Corps. The American air units that saw action at the Front were equipped with French and British aeroplanes because America did not produce any machines good enough to use during the war. America's best contribution to the Allies was men.

Major John W. F. M. Huffer, who was born in Paris of American parents, was one of the Americans who enlisted in the Foreign Legion and served in many ways during the years 1914–1917 before America entered the war. Huffer joined the Foreign Legion in September 1915 and was transferred to the *Service d'Aéronautique* the first of 1916. From the spring of 1916 to the beginning of 1918, he flew with several French fighter and reconnaissance *escadrilles* on both the Western Front and in Italy. When the U.S.A.S. began to shape up in France early in 1918, Huffer was one of the experienced men ready to transfer into it to give his green countrymen the benefit of his experience. He was commissioned a Major and assigned to the command of the 94th Aero Squadron. The 94th and the 95th, the first American fighter squadrons in the field, were based near Toul and formed the nucleus of the First Pursuit Group. Major Huffer commanded the 94th from March to May 1918, held a staff job for a time, then returned to combat as the Commanding Officer of the 93rd Aero Squadron from July to the end of the war in November 1918. He won the French *Croix de Guerre,* the American Distinguished Service Cross and survived the war with seven confirmed victories.

Shortly after Major Huffer took command of the 94th, there arrived at the field to serve as "special instructor" the star of the *Escadrille Lafayette,* Raoul Lufbery.

Lufbery was the name of an old English family which had emigrated to America in the eighteenth century. Edward Lufbery, one of the descendants of that family, was born in New York in 1854. In 1876 he settled in France and obtained a position as chief chemist for an industrial rubber concern. There he married and there his son, Gervais Raoul Victor Lufbery, was born 14 March 1885. At the age of twelve Raoul was compelled by disastrous reversals in the family fortunes to start working. In 1905 he slipped out of the house one day with three hundred hard-earned francs in his pocket and set out on a trip "around the world." He took any odd job he could find to stretch his slim resources and thus worked his way to Algiers, Tunis, Cairo, Constantinople, Athens. In June 1906, a few months past his twenty-first birthday, he felt obliged to make a permanent decision with regard to his citizenship, for he was due to be called up soon by the French army for his compulsory service. He visited the French consul in Cairo and formally declared his intention to adopt his father's American citizenship. That done, he resumed his wandering—Bucharest, Budapest, Vienna, Hamburg. From Hamburg he sailed for New York, arriving there in May 1907.

Lufbery banged around the United States, ranging up into Canada and down into Mexico. In San Francisco he came to a dead stop and stared out over the immense Pacific. What now? One day on the street an army recruiter approached him with an enthusiastic description of the pleasures of army life. Lufbery listened politely but without much interest until he heard the magic name Hawaii. He was promptly enrolled in the 20th Infantry Regiment and in a detachment of fifty men and a handful of officers landed in Honolulu in December 1908. He served there until March 1910 when he was sent to Manila, and in July 1911 was given an honorable discharge. He started traveling again on his mustering-out pay. He drifted on to India, and in Calcutta he met one of the great French pioneer aviators, Marc Pourpe.

Pourpe, born in 1889 in Lorient, spent a year each at Harrow and Heidelberg before entering the Chaptal College in Paris. His first big foreign adventure was a jaunt to Australia as assistant and mechanic to a rich sports-

Musée de l'Air / Paris

Pourpe.

man who had purchased a Wright "B" Flyer and planned to do a bit of barnstorming. Pourpe learned to fly "down under" and, characteristically, induced the aborigines to teach him to throw the boomerang. Back in France during the winter of 1910–1911 he took a position as flying instructor at an aerodrome near Nice, then in April 1911 created a sensation by flying in a storm at Boulogne-sur-Mer, something that just wasn't attempted in those days. The following year, while serving as a test pilot for the Tellier aeroplane company, he cracked up and only narrowly escaped death. For some unknown reason his machine dived straight into the ground from an altitude of perhaps two hundred feet. He managed to recover, but the machine dived again, this time from so low down that there was no hope of pulling out. At the last second Pourpe scrambled out of the cockpit and sprawled on the wing. Apparently this desperate action saved him, for the wing crumpled up and let him down gently while the fuselage was smashed. He suffered a dislocated knee, a broken ankle and a few scratches. He was out of the hospital and flying again in a few months. In August 1912 he attempted to make the first cross-country flight from Paris to Berlin, but was forced to give up because of foul weather. The honor went to another pioneer named Edmond Audemars.

Pourpe joined partners with two rich friends, brothers from Marseille named Georges and Charles Verminck, and the three planned a barnstorming tour of the exotic East. Pourpe designed four packing crates, in three of which could be stowed three dismantled Blériot monoplanes with spare tires and propellers, while the fourth was rigged up as a machine shop and in it were stowed, among other things, a tent hangar, a spare Gnôme rotary engine, steel tubing, sheet aluminum and enough wood to build at least five other aeroplanes.

In Calcutta a young man approached the troupe and asked if it might not be able to use a handyman. Pourpe hired him on the spot; it was, of course, Raoul Lufbery. In April 1913 Georges Verminck was killed in a crack-up in Cambodia; the partners broke up, but Pourpe and Lufbery decided to carry on. For the next several months, until the end of August 1913, they operated all over French Indo-China, Pourpe doing all the flying in their aging Blériot, *La Curieuse,* and Lufbery nursing the machine along and taking care of all the ground arrangements. By the time they returned to France in September Pourpe had flown over 10,000 miles and was regarded by aviators as the unchallenged "champion of colonial aviation."

With the outbreak of war, all the famous pioneers of aviation offered their services to their governments, but so little provision was made for aviation in the great general plans that it took some time to absorb them. Pourpe was sent to Longvic about the end of August 1914 for a brief course on the needs of military aeronautics and in September was posted to *Escadrille M-S 23*, stationed near Nancy, in which Roland Garros was already flying. It was arranged for Lufbery to enter the First Regiment of the Foreign

Legion, whence he was immediately detached for aviation and posted to M-S 23 to be Pourpe's mechanic.

Pourpe, a southerner by birth, suffered when the weather turned cold. He flew thirty grueling missions of from two-and-a-half to three hours in freezing temperatures, was wounded and began to feel fatigue and depression. By the beginning of December 1914 his mental state was not good, and bitterness aggravated it. He was the only one in the squadron whose machine had been hit by antiaircraft fire, who had himself been wounded, and who had not yet been promoted. Besides this, there was a residue of pardonable peacetime bitterness because he had never received one iota of recognition from the French Government for his pioneering flying in the colonies. The cold itself was the worst enemy, however. It caused him horrible discomfort, and it may be that it was the cold that finally killed him.

On 2 December 1914, a bitterly cold and windy day, he flew a long-distance reconnaissance with an artillery observer named *Lieutenant* Vauglin. His *Parasol* was heard flying overhead when they returned from the mission, but owing to dense masses of cloud could not be seen until suddenly it dropped through the clouds in a tailspin. Whether or not Pourpe tried to recover was impossible to judge. Those watching from the ground saw his machine spin all the way down without once being checked and smash into the hard-frozen earth with terrific violence. Those that knew him said he could have handled an aeroplane under any circumstances, but that he was probably so cold and frozen he was simply unable to maneuver.

The same day Lufbery asked to be transferred for flying training. In May 1915 he was sent to the flying school at Chartres and graduated on 29 July. He was assigned to *Escadrille* VB. 102 on 7 October and flew his first mission three days later. His chief emotion on this occasion, he afterwards said, was a kind of pride that the enemy should go to so much trouble for him, for he was "saluted" by their antiaircraft fire all the way to the target and back.

Lufbery flew steadily through the winter of 1915–1916, but began to feel that he could do better than to push around the big busses in a bombing squadron. When he was approached, on the basis of his American citizenship, as a candidate for the *Escadrille Lafayette,* he decided this was just the opportunity he was looking for and requested a transfer to fighters. The request was granted, he was sent for conversion training to Nieuport single-seaters in April 1916, and joined the *Lafayette* stationed near Verdun on 24 May. He flew several patrols before he had his first fight on 4 June. On that occasion he spotted a photographic two-seater escorted by an *Eindecker* which at the moment happened to be separated from its charge by some little distance. He rushed the *Eindecker* hoping to take its pilot by surprise. Instead, the German eluded his attack and put a burst into his Nieuport. After some sparring, Lufbery managed to fire one burst at the *Eindecker,* but his gun jammed when it had fired only fifteen rounds. The enemy pilot, apparently satisfied that Lufbery was no longer going to be a nuisance, went on about his business without pressing his advantage and Lufbery flew home disgusted with himself.

He took a personal interest in his bus and his guns, and he worked on both his marksmanship and his tactics. His guns rarely jammed and his motors rarely packed up, and his squadron mates said they would rather have a secondhand Lufbery machine than a new one any day. On 31 July 1916, after sixteen inconclusive combats, he scored his first victory with a diving attack on an *Eindecker* which after one burst fell in a spin and was seen to crash by French troops in the front-line trenches.

On 8 August Lufbery and Sergeant James McConnell, one of the original members of the *Lafayette,* took off together on a patrol to the northeast of Verdun, between Douaumont and Vaux. At about 12,000 feet Lufbery throttled back and cruised along easily, keeping his neck swiveling constantly as he searched about him for enemy machines. Jim McConnell was doing the same thing, and the two were so intent on searching the sky that they lost contact with each other and drifted a considerable distance apart. Lufbery soon spotted a machine about 3000 feet below him and headed toward the French lines. It was painted a very dark color and hard to see against the dark earth at that distance. Lufbery cut his motor and went into a curving dive which brought him out below and behind the machine and on the way down he perceived that it was indeed a German two-seater. It was a good set-up for an attack, and after one more prudent look around to make sure that he wasn't biting on a baited hook, he gunned his motor and began closing the distance. The pilot or the observer in the machine ahead finally spotted him, but too late. As the two-seater swerved to the right Lufbery opened fire, coming so close that he had to break hard to the left to avoid a collision. As he rolled over and recovered, Lufbery looked below him to judge the effect of his attack on the two-seater. To his amazement, the machine now appeared to be completely white. He raised his goggles to get a better look and saw that the machine was tumbling wildly and that at that moment was upside down so that its belly was uppermost, displaying its light-camouflaged undersurfaces. It began throwing out smoke and was soon burning furiously.

Just at the moment of Lufbery's attack, Jim McConnell had turned in the direction of the two machines and had seen the German start to fall and burst into flame. He briefly lost sight of it as it went down and saw it again skimming the ground over no-man's-land. Still trailing a thick black cloud of smoke it finally hit the ground just short of the French trenches and disintegrated.

The victory was confirmed by the ground observers by the time Lufbery landed. At lunch after the patrol, while Lufbery was receiving everyone's congratulations, McConnell heard him mutter, "Poor bastards." To get his four victories Lufbery had flown one hundred thirty hours on patrol and had had twenty-nine combats.

A few days later Jim McConnell was injured when he cracked up in a forced landing. His back was severely sprained and never quite the same afterward. He was hospitalized twice with the injury and insisted on returning to combat before he was fit. He was so troubled with pain and stiffness that when he was shot down and killed in March 1917, his squadron mates all conjectured it was because he was unable to turn and look about and so was easily surprised by an enemy pilot coming up behind him.

About the end of November 1916 Lufbery received a new Spad 7 and turned in his Nieuport. He was very pleased with his new machine once he had it tuned up and squared away to his satisfaction. He scored his sixth victory with it on 27 December, his victim according to some sources being a twenty-two-year-old native of Wilhemshaven, *Leutnant* Gustav Leffers, who was flying an Albatros D II with *Jasta 1*. Leffers was one of the few

Eindecker aces, had won nine confirmed victories and the *Pour le Mérite*. Lufbery was awarded the Legion of Honor.

At the end of 1917, Lufbery, because of his experience and his American citizenship, was offered a commission in the U.S.A.S. He accepted, and to his dismay was promptly sent to the U.S. Air Instruction Center at Issoudun. There he fidgeted behind a desk and bombarded his superiors with requests for a transfer back to a combat squadron. Finally he was sent to Major Huffer's 94th Aero Squadron at Toul in April 1918 to serve as special instructor.

French ace Raoul Lufbery at the wheel of an Hispano Suiza roadster.

U.S. Air Force

Two other veterans of the *Lafayette* had now donned American uniforms and joined the 94th, James Norman Hall and David McKelvey Peterson, both of whom had scored one victory with the unit, and both of whom now held the rank of Captain in the U.S.A.S.

Peterson was a tall, quiet Pennsylvanian who whistled but could not carry a tune. He survived the war with five confirmed victories, but was killed in an accident a few months after the Armistice.

Hall was a rather rare bird, a fighter pilot with a college degree. Not that pilots were not susceptible to education, but most of them joined the service when they were teen-agers. When the war broke out, Hall was on a bicycle trip through England, he promptly enlisted in the 9th Battalion of the Royal Fusiliers. He spent most of 1915 in the trenches at Loos and Messines, was discharged, returned to the United States, then returned to France in the summer of 1916 and enlisted in the *Service d'Aéronautique*. His first victory was the last scored by the *Escadrille Lafayette*. On 1 January 1918, he and *Lieutenant* William Thaw, one of the charter members of the outfit, went out on a high patrol early in the afternoon. The ground was covered with snow and the air was bitterly cold, but the sky was clear save for broken and towering masses of dazzling white cloud. As so often happened, the two got separated. Hall continued on alone for a time and finally spotted a far-off speck against the shining clouds. Supposing this to be Thaw's machine he headed toward it, climbing slightly to put himself above it. As he drew close enough to make out the silhouette he was startled to realize that the other machine was an Albatros single-seater. Its pilot was looping, rolling and contour-chasing over the tops of the clouds, apparently lost in the joy of flying and the overwhelming beauty of the aerial scene. Hall said later that he allowed himself one brief second to reflect that here was no doubt a man who had forgotten why he was up there. Hall easily took this man by surprise and sent him down literally with his wings shot off. One of the wings fluttered down in French territory. The enemy pilot was just as dead as if he'd put up a stiff fight, but Hall felt no elation over his victory.

Among the new men who came in to make up the strength of the 94th were Alan Winslow, Douglas Campbell and Edward Vernon Rickenbacker. They had the distinction of being the first American-trained pilots to see action, but they were patiently coached by Lufbery first, and Lufbery's coaching took up where their training left off. Rickenbacker, who survived the war with twenty-six confirmed victories, making him the top-scoring American ace, eventually commanded the 94th. The next highest-scoring American ace was Captain (now Lt. Col.) William C. Lambert who scored twenty-two victories in Hawker's old squadron during 1918 when it was known as No. 24 Squadron R.A.F. Lambert flew solely with the British and his name usually does not appear on American ace lists.

The Nieuport 28 with which the 94th Aero Squadron and the first American squadrons generally were equipped was quite different from previous mounts from the Nieuport stable except that a rotary engine was once again used, this one the fairly powerful nine-cylinder 160-horsepower Gnôme-Rhône. The fuselage of the 28 was rounded in cross-section, as opposed to the usual slab-sided Nieuport look, and the wings were roughly equal in span and chord, as opposed to the sesquiplane layout with "V" struts. The ailerons were located in the lower wing. The 28 was a streamlined, elegant aeroplane, very maneuverable and easy to fly, but it developed a serious weakness soon after it was introduced at the Front. In a prolonged dive or during violent maneuvering the fabric on the wings sometimes peeled off. Apparently condensation, resulting from normal daily climatic change, attacked the glue of the plywood leading edge causing the plywood to come unstuck. The loosened plywood worked against the wing covering, putting a severe strain on it so that the fabric might split from the overload it took in diving or rough handling. Once the fabric was split, the slipstream got under it and ripped it away. The problem was a critical one, but fortunately few fatalities resulted from it. By the summer of 1918 when the problem was licked, most United States squadrons had switched to Spads. The United States purchased about three hundred 28's and it has the honor of being the bus with which the first "all-American" victories were achieved.

The first score for the 94th was a simultaneous double victory on 14 April 1918. As Alan Winslow and Douglas Campbell were putting in a few hours on "stand by" on a foggy, misty morning, two German fighters were spotted cruising near the field by ground observers who telephoned the news to the squadron H.Q. Winslow and Campbell immediately got their motors

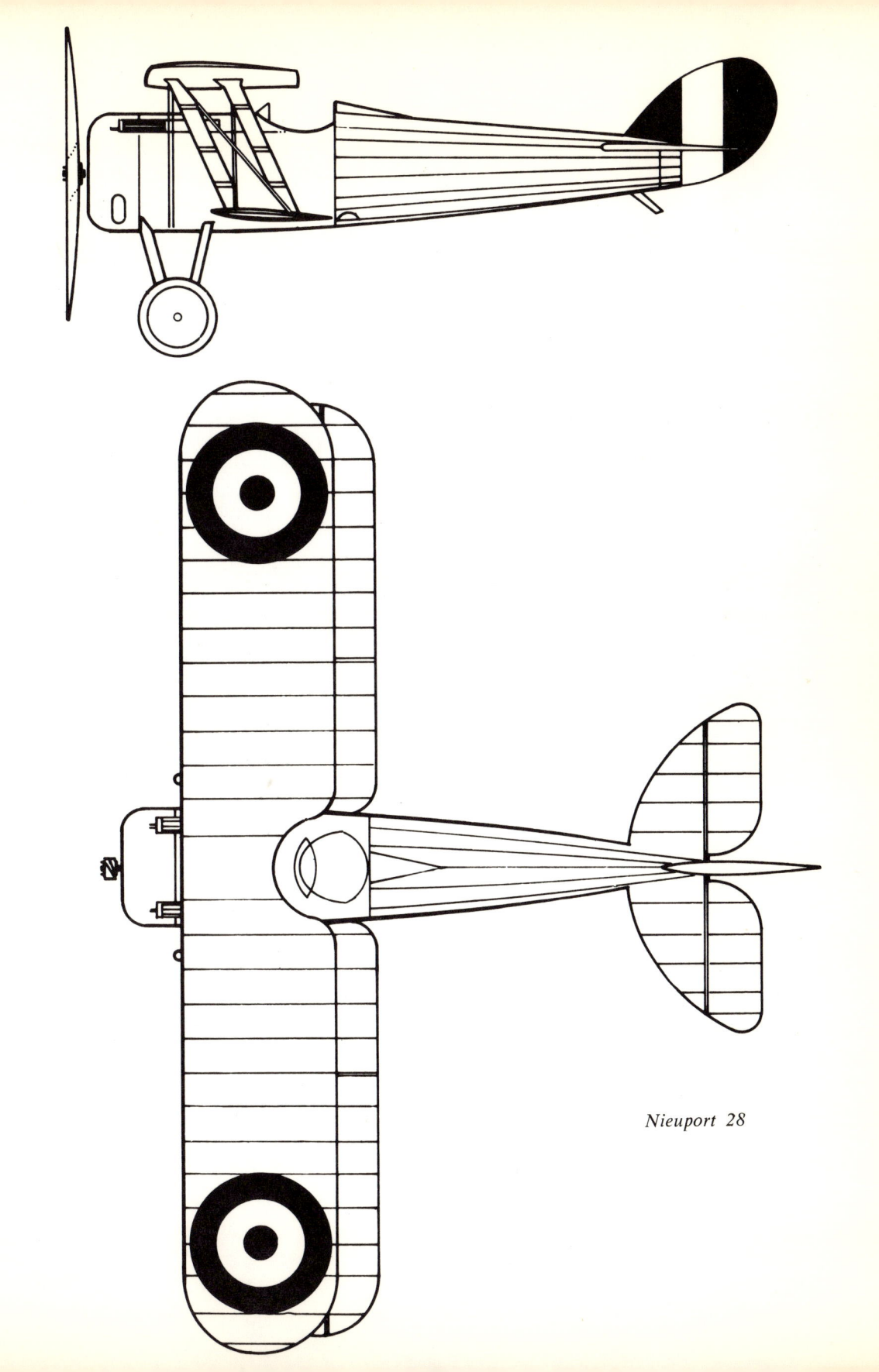

Nieuport 28

U. S. Air Force

Nieuport 28

started up and took off just as the two enemy machines appeared out of the mist near the aerodrome. Winslow, with Campbell right behind him, made good use of the mist to come up behind one of the German machines, an Albatros D V, and open fire from close range. At that same moment the other, a Pfalz D III, came up behind Campbell and opened fire on him. Campbell threw his machine violently to one side. After a moment of sparring, he got underneath his opponent and put a burst into his motor at close range, while out of the corner of his eye he saw Winslow's opponent go down.

It was all over very quickly. In a little over three minutes both Winslow and Campbell were back on the ground, each having gotten his man. The German fighters had crash-landed at either end of the aerodrome within a few hundred yards of the hangars, and both German pilots were taken alive.

On 7 May Jim Hall led Rickenbacker and Lieutenant Edward Green on a patrol in the course of which they encountered four German fighters a few miles the other side of the lines. As they held the height advantage, Hall and his two men did not hesitate to attack. Rickenbacker got on the tail of one of the enemy machines and gave it a good burst, but dared not hold on long enough to make sure of a victory for fear somebody would come up behind him and nail him. He broke away and looked around in time to see Green pour a burst into another enemy machine which immediately spun down out of control. Rickenbacker then looked around for Hall, but he was nowhere to be seen and the other German fighters had cleared out. The sky was empty except for Green's aeroplane, so Rickenbacker closed up to it and together they flew home.

As soon as they landed, Rickenbacker ran over to where Green was parking his bus to ask if he had seen what happened to Hall, but before he could speak Green cried out that he had seen Hall go down with the fabric torn off his upper wing. He also told Rickenbacker that he had seen the aeroplane that Rickenbacker had attacked and which he had not had time to follow fall in flames. Rickenbacker was amazed; he had no idea he had gotten that one. Additional confirmation came after the war when they met Jim Hall again. Hall had nearly been finished by the Nieuport weakness, for he had fallen a long way out of control when his wings peeled. He had, however, been able to recover and straighten out, after which he set a course for home and hoped to nurse his machine to friendly territory. He was too low down for safety, unfortunately, and being easy meat for the German antiaircraft artillery, had taken a direct hit in the motor. The shell failed to explode, but it smashed the motor and his 28 dropped out from under him. He piled up near Pagny-sur-Moselle, suffering a broken nose, but doubly lucky to have come through at all after having lost his wings and being hit by antiaircraft gunfire (popularly known as "Archie" by pilots). The Germans told Hall that two of their machines had been shot down in the fight. Thus the Germans confirmed Rickenbacker's victory themselves, but he never claimed it and it was never credited to him. After the war Hall settled in Tahiti where in collaboration with Charles B. Nordhoff, a former fighter pilot himself, he wrote the *Bounty Trilogy*.

After Rickenbacker's victim went down in flames, the men asked Lufbery what a pilot should do if his bus caught fire in the air. Lufbery may have given different answers to this question at different times, for some say he advised sticking with the aeroplane. Some pilots had been known to bring off successful crash landings in burning machines by sideslipping all the way down, thus fanning the flames off to one side and away from the cockpit. Others remember Lufbery saying that he would never go down a flamer, but whether he meant that he didn't believe it would ever happen to him or that he had some other solution in mind is impossible to say.

On Sunday, 19 May 1918, at about ten o'clock in the morning, a big German two-seater droned over the aerodrome, probably on a photography mission. Antiaircraft guns opened up, but did not succeed in bringing it down or chasing it away. Major Lufbery jumped into a Nieuport and took off after the enemy machine. The men of the squadron expected that this was going to be a short and snappy interception. They watched as Lufbery made several attacks without any apparent effect, then suddenly to their great horror saw flames swirl back over the cowling of the Nieuport. As the aeroplane burned furiously, they saw a small dot fall away from it—Lufbery had jumped. Whether he had thought it out or not no one knows; it can only be said that when the end finally came it was as he had said it would be. He didn't go down a flamer.

As had happened in Boelcke's squadron and in Hawker's squadron, and in a hundred other squadrons, a forceful personality, a valuable and experienced man was gone forever and his comrades could do nothing about it but carry on.

By the end of May both Campbell and Rickenbacker were aces. On 6 June 1918, Campbell was wounded in an attack on a German two-seater. He began his attack with a diving pass and worked the enemy machine from 18,000 down to 3000 feet, but the Hun pilot was good and his maneuvering kept his own rear gunner clear to shoot, so Campbell was obliged to keep a respectful distance. Seeing a long tape breezing out behind the rear cockpit, and supposing that such a length of empty belt meant the gunner must be out of ammunition, Campbell closed in for the kill. His intended victim was still full of fight, however, and although he may indeed have been low on ammunition, he had enough left nearly to turn the tables on Campbell. As the American finished one pass and rolled away, the German gunner poured a burst into his Nieuport right behind the cockpit and a large piece of shrapnel buried itself in Campbell's back. He immediately broke off and headed for home. The wound was not critical, but the first all-American ace was out of action for the rest of the war.

On 25 September 1918, Rickenbacker took over command of the squadron, which had by this time switched to Spads. On the same day, he scored a double victory for which he was later awarded the Congressional Medal of Honor. High over Étain on a solo patrol he spotted two German two-seaters escorted by five Fokker D VII's. He eyed the Fokkers warily, not only

Rickenbacker

U. S. Air Force

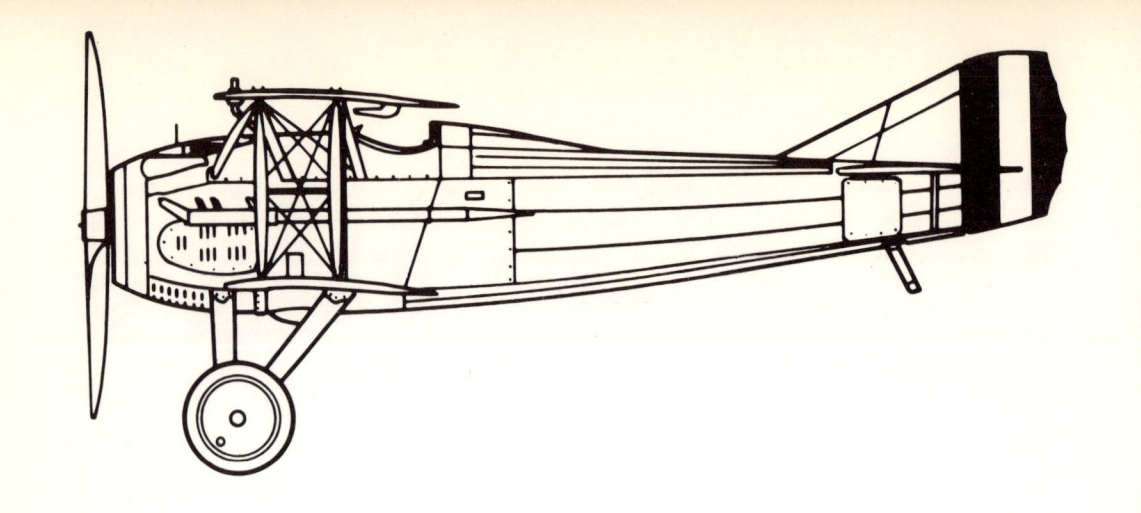

Spad 13

because there were five of them, but because they were dangerous adversaries. The D VII was the only Fokker fighter to see service in large numbers, about 3000 of them being produced for first-line *Jastas* between April 1918 and the end of the war in November. For the British and the French who had been fighting Albatros single-seaters for years, the Fokker D VII was just one more enemy ship to contend with, but the Americans were still new to the war and this was the enemy fighter they most frequently encountered. It made a big impression on them. Rickenbacker worked himself into a good position above the enemy machines and in the sun, and because he was alone, he figured he had not been spotted. He went into a dive, planning to get the last man in the Fokker formation and then escape by zooming, since the Spad 13 could outclimb the D VII. With luck he could hit and run before they knew what hit them. He caught his man completely by surprise with a long burst at close range, the pilot slumped in his seat and his machine dropped in a spin. The other Fokkers, instead of ganging up on Rickenbacker, scattered all over the sky. With the escort thus

Spad 13

U. S. Air Force

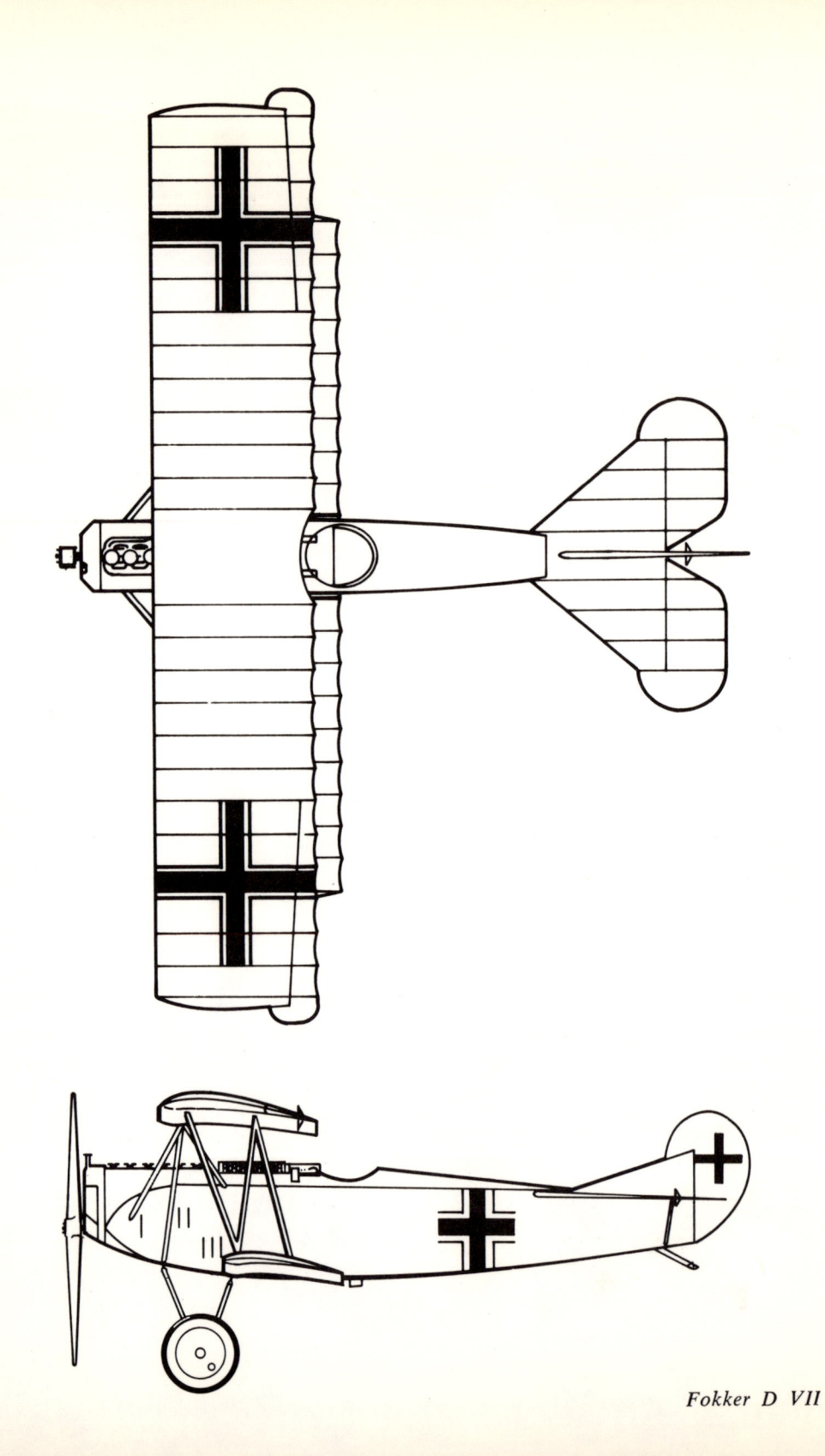

Fokker D VII

Wm. E. Morse, Jr.

Fokker D VII

broken up, Rickenbacker threw caution to the winds and went for the two-seaters. They were not so easy. The pilots were good and they maneuvered together so that their gunners could cover each other. Rickenbacker was several times forced to break away when they sent bullets streaking past his face. As they were getting deeper into German territory all the time, there was the danger that the Fokkers would pull themselves together and come at him all at once, so he decided that he would have one last try for one of the two-seaters and then clear out. He suddenly saw a move open to him and took immediate advantage of it. The two-seaters, he perceived, were flying parallel and close to each other. He quickly attacked from diagonally ahead of the nearer machine so that it masked the fire of the other gunner, and the gunner of the nearer machine found his fire blocked by his own wings. As he closed in, Rickenbacker started shooting. The two-seater went right through a stream of lead and burst into flames. Rickenbacker opened his throttle and headed for home, leaving behind the Fokkers who returned to the scene too late.

Musée de l'Air / Paris

Roland Garros

AFTER THREE YEARS of captivity, Roland Garros escaped from the citadel of Magdeburg and succeeded in returning to France by way of Holland in February 1918. A lot had happened in the years since Garros had introduced his armored-propeller Morane on 1 April 1915. Aero engines had gone up in horsepower from eighty to one hundred to two hundred twenty or three hundred or even four hundred. Aeroplanes could now fly at speeds of up to two hundred miles per hour and attain altitudes of over 20,000 feet. The R.A.F. had a fleet of bombers that was ready to fly all the way to Germany and back from bases in England.

"I am a novice now!" Garros said in a newspaper interview. "What am I beside those who had not even flown before my capture? I used to say that the progress which would be achieved in three years would surpass imagination, but I never thought I would be the first victim of that progress . . ."

On his return to active duty Garros had literally to start over again and was sent to Pau in southern France to attend the combat aerobatic school. Assigned to Spa 26 under the command of *Capitaine* de Sévin, Garros threw himself into his flying. He was desperately eager to achieve some spectacular success to make up for all his lost time, but he was so far behind in experience that he had little chance of catching up. As he himself said, he was a victim of progress. On 5 October 1918, the fourth anniversary of the first aerial victory of all time, that of Frantz and Quénault, Garros went out on patrol and failed to return. Fears of his death were confirmed when the Swiss newspapers on 19 October picked up a dispatch released through the Wolff Telegraph Bureau, Germany's major news agency: ". . . the aviator Garros was mortally brought down in the German lines on 5 October. Before the war, Garros was one of the best-known French aviators. He was taken prisoner 18 April 1915, and escaped in February 1918. Upon his return he was first occupied in the construction of aeroplanes and later returned to the Front."

Some days later, French troops entering Vouziers found his grave in the southwest corner of the civil cemetery there.

*   *   *

Squadron Insignias

Every squadron—on both sides—had its own insignia, which was emblazoned proudly on the fuselages of its airplanes. These are some examples of insignias used by various French squadrons.

Groupe de Combat Spa-26

Escadrille de Corps d'Armée C.27

Spa-68

Groupe de Combat Spa-Lafayette

Avion de Bombardement B.M. 119

Avion de Bombardement S.R. 120

Escadrille de Chasse Spa-62

Escadrille de Corps d'Armée G.56

A.R. 22 Corps d'Armée

Escadrille de Corps d'Armée A.R. 58

A.R. 201

Corpes d'Armee Sop. 13

Escadrille de Chasse Spa-97

RECOMMENDED READING

First and foremost in any aviation bibliography is the *Cross & Cockade Journal*. This publication of The Society of World War I Aero Historians is sincerely recommended to anyone who wishes to learn more about the colorful aeroplanes and personalities of aviation's most exciting era. Every issue has drawings, photographs, and articles covering all aspects of the air war of 1914-1918, plus translations of otherwise unobtainable French and German material. Some of the articles are by the veterans themselves. Aviation enthusiasts are urged to send all inquiries to the Business Manager, Cross & Cockade, 10443 South Memphis Avenue, Whittier, California, 90604. An impressive series of aviation titles has been produced by Harleyford Publications, Limited, of Letchworth, Hertfordshire, England. Some of the outstanding World War I titles of the past ten years are:

Von Richthofen and the Flying Circus, Nowarra and Brown.
Fokker—The Man and the Aircraft, Hegener.
Fighter Aircraft of the 1914-1918 War, Lamberton and Cheesman.
Air Aces of the 1914-1918 War, Robertson *et al.*

The following books are all highly recommended:

Hawker, V. C., Tyrrel M. Hawker. London, The Mitre Press, 1965.
Fighting the Flying Circus, Edward V. Rickenbacker. Garden City, Doubleday & Company, Inc., 1965.
Fokker: The Creative Years, A. R. Weyl. London, Putnam and Company, Limited, 1965.
German Aircraft of the First World War, Peter Gray and Owen Thetford. London, Putnam and Company, Limited, 1962.
Heroes and Aeroplanes of the Great War 1914-1918, Joseph Phelan, New York, Grosset & Dunlap, Inc., 1966.
More extensive than the book at hand is the author's *The Fighters,* New York, Grosset & Dunlap, Inc., 1965.

INDEX

A

Aerial reconnaissance, early use of, 18
Air fighting, age of, 32
Albatros, 105, 143
Albatros C III, 92
Albatros D I, 87–90
Albatros D II, 95, 97, 133
Albatros D III, 97, 101
Albatros D V, 118, 138
Albatros single seaters, 87
Albatros Works, 87
Andrews, J. O., 77, 95
Armaments, first use of, in planes, 31–35
Audemars, Edmond, 130
Aviatik, 34, 39, 62, 64

B

Barès, 67, 69
B.E., 103
B.E. 2c, 93
B.E. 2d, 77
Bébé, 60–63, 69, 82
Becker, Hermann, 114–115; cited for *Pour le Mérite*, 73
Biddle, Charles J., 18–23
Biplanes, B class, German, 44
Biplanes, C class, German, 44
Birkigt, Marc, 83
Blériot, Louis, 18, 24
Blériot XI, 28
Blériot flying schools, 18–23
Blériot monoplane, 130
Boelcke, Oswald: 42–44, 90–94, 97, 140; death of, 94–95; and Fokker Eindecker, 56–59; awarded *Pour le Mérite*, 59, 94; strategy influence of, 57
Boelcke, Wilhelm, 42

Bonnet, and invention of parachute, 24
Bozon-Verduraz, Benjamin, 101
Bristol Baby, 74
Brocard, 80–82
Brown, A. Roy, 117–122
Buie, Robert, 122
Butler, C. H., 117–122

C

Camel, 103–107
Campbell, Douglas, 135–141
Carlin, 24
Collishaw, Raymond, 111

D

de Beauvricourt, 44
de Bernis, 40
Delage, Gustave, 60
de Meux, Alfred de Laage, 125
de Rose, Tricornot, 67–68, 76
de Sevin, 147
D.H.2: 75–77, 94–96, 107; compared with D I, 87
Dr I, 112

E

Eindecker: 52–57, 65, 67, 72–73, 77, 132; compared to Bébé, 60; withdrawal of, 87
Escadrille Américaine, formation of, 123
Evans, W. J., 122

F

Farman, Maurice, 40, 65
Faure, Andre, 31–32

F.E.: 103; 2b, 72, 93–94
Fee. *See* F.E. 2b
Fighter aviation, development of, 67–69
Fliegerabteilungen, 42–44
Fokker, Anthony Herman Gerard, 28, 51–52, 111–112
Fokker, craft, 73, 105
Fokker Dr I. *See* Dr I
Fokker D VII, 141
Fokker Eindecker. *See* Eindecker
Fokker M.5. *See* M.5
Fokker Triplane, 103, 111–115
Frantz, Joseph, 32–35, 147

G

Garros, Roland: 36–39, 51, 60, 130, 147; death of, 147; and single-seater fighter, 36–39
Girard, 42
Green, Edward, 139
Gros, Edmund, 123
Guerder, 80
Guynemer, George: 80–85; death of, 101; and Legion of Honor, 82–100

H

Halberstadt D II, 87
Halberstadt Flying School, 42
Hall, Bert, 125
Hall, James Norman, 125, 135, 139–140
Haviland, Willis B., 125
Hawker, H. C., 74
Hawker, Lanoe George, 74–76, 94–96, 140; death of, 96; awarded Victoria Cross, 75
Heurtaux, Alfred, 100
Hispano Suiza motors, 83–85
Hotchkiss, early use of, 35–36
Huffer, John W. F. M., 127–128, 134

I

Immelmann, Max: 56–59, 72–73, 97; death of, 73; awarded *Pour le Mérite,* 59, 94; strategy influence of, 57–58

J

Jagdstaffein, formation of, 90. *See also Jasta*
Jasta, Boelcke's, 90–94
Johnson, Charles C., 125
Jones, Henry S., 125
Justinus, Bruno, 64–65

K

Kampfeinsitzer-Kommandos, 69, 90
Kastner, 56–57
K.E.K. *See* Kampfeinsitzer Kommandos
Kirmaier, Stephan, 95
Knight, 94
Kreutzer, Martin, 111

L

Lafayette Escadrille, 123–125, 131–132
Lambert, William C., 136
Le Boutillier, O. C., 117–122
Leffers, Gustav, awarded *Pour le Mérite,* 133
Lewis gun: on *Bébé,* 60; on Bristol Baby, 74–75; and S.E.5, 105
Loewenhardt, 114
Lovell, Walter, 125
Lufbery, Edward, 128
Lufbery, Raoul: 125–135; death of, 140; awarded Legion of Honor, 134
Luftstreitkrafte, 97
Luftwaffe, 64

M

M.5, Fokker: 29; with armament, 51–54
McConnell, James, 132–133
McCubbin, 72
Marr, Kenneth, 125
Masson, Didier, 125
May, Wilfred R., 117–122
Mellersh, F. J. W., 117–122
Military aviation, beginning of, 14
Moranes, 28, 80, 83
Morane-Saulnier N, 36
Morane-Saulnier *Parasols. See* Parasols

N

Navarre, Jean, 40–42, 69–72
Navarre, Pierre, 40–42, 72
Niéport, Edouard de, 60
Nieuport: 83, 132; compared with D I, 87
Nieuport 28, 136, 139
Nieuport Bébé. *See* Bébé
Nordhoff, Charles B., 140

O

Otto Flying School, 64

P

Parabellum: 60; trials of, 51; use of, 44
Parachute: invention of, 24; use of, 24–27
Parasols, 40–42, 44, 80, 131
Parsons, Edwin C., 125
Pégoud, Adolphe: 24–28, 51, 60–62; strategy influence of, 58
Penguin, as training craft, 18, 60
Petain, Henri Phillipe, on air superiority, 67
Peterson, David McKelvey, 125, 135
Pfalz D III, 138
Platz, Reinhold, 111–112
Popkin, C. B., 122
Pourpe, Marc, 128–131
Prince, Norman, 123

Q

Quénault, Louis, 32–35, 147

R

R.E., 103
Reconnaissance flights, early, described, 43–44
Redgate, O. W., 117
R.F.C. *See* Royal Flying Corps
Rickenbacker, Edward V.; 135, 139–145; awarded Congressional Medal of Honor, 141–145
Rockwell, Kiffin, 125
Royal Aero Club, 74

Royal Aircraft Factory, 103
Royal Air Force, origins of, 117
Royal Flying Corps: and arming of aeroplanes, 31; composition of, 31; and F.E. 2b., 72–73; offence of, 95. *See also* Royal Air Force

S

S.7, 83–85
S.13, 83–85
Salmond, John, 117
Saundby, Robert H. M. S., 95
Saulnier, Raymond, 36
Savary biplane, 34
Schubert, 87
S.E.5, 103–105
Service d'Aeronautique: 40, 60, 68; and arming of aeroplanes, 31–32; composition of, 31; training flights of, 18
Single-seater fighters, origins of, 36
Societé pour Aviation et ses Derives, 83
Sopwith Camel. *See* Camel
Sopwith Triplane, 111, 114
Spad, 105, 115, 136, 141
Spad 7: 133; compared with D I, 87
Spad 13, 143
Spad single-seaters, 82–85

T

Thaw, William, 125, 135
Thelen, 87

U

U.S.A.S., 127, 134
Udet, Ernst, 26, 64–65, 114

V

Vauglin, 131
Verdun, battle of, 67
Vergnette, 36
Verminck, Charles, 130
Verminck, Georges, 130

Vickers gun: on Camel, 107; on S.E.5, 105; on Spad 7, 85
Voisin, Charles, 31
Voisin, Gabriel, 15–16, 31–32
Voisin Aeroplane Company, 31
von Falkenhayn, 29
von Richthofen, Albrecht, 91
von Richthofen, Manfred: 91–92, 96–97, 114, 118–122; awarded *Pour le Mérite*, 97
von Richthofen, Wolfram, 118
von Schleich, Eduard, 26
von Wuehlisch, 44
Voss, 114

W

Waller, 72
Winslow, Alan, 135–139
Wolseley Viper, and S.E.5a, 105

A NOTE ABOUT THE AUTHOR

THOMAS R. FUNDERBURK, a native of Indiana, spent two years in the Marine Corps and later graduated from Indiana University. He lives in New York City with his wife and daughter, and has traveled extensively in Europe, seeking rare and out of print books on the Great War and interviewing the surviving airmen.

Years of painstaking research and correspondence with World War I authorities went into the preparation of this book, Mr. Funderburk has personally talked with many of the men who fought in the war, and they have given him permission to use their eyewitness accounts, diaries and photographs.

Mr. Funderburk is also the author of THE FIGHTERS: *The Men and Machines of the First Air War. Air Progress* magazine called it ". . . a genuine historical document packed with primary source material gathered in personal interviews with the men who won the air battles of 1914–1918 . . . the next best thing to having been on the Western Front."

4⁵⁰